THE COAL INDUSTRY
IN THE
LLYNFI VALLEY

THE COAL INDUSTRY
IN THE
LLYNFI VALLEY

DAVID LEWIS

TEMPUS

First published 2006

Tempus Publishing Limited
The Mill, Brimscombe Port,
Stroud, Gloucestershire, GL5 2QG
www.tempus-publishing.com

© David Lewis, 2006

The right of David Lewis to be identified as the Author
of this work has been asserted in accordance with the
Copyrights, Designs and Patents Act 1988.

All rights reserved. No part of this book may be reprinted
or reproduced or utilised in any form or by any electronic,
mechanical or other means, now known or hereafter invented,
including photocopying and recording, or in any information
storage or retrieval system, without the permission in writing
from the Publishers.

British Library Cataloguing in Publication Data.
A catalogue record for this book is available from the British Library.

ISBN 0 7524 3872 7

Typesetting and origination by Tempus Publishing Limited
Printed in Great Britain

CONTENTS

Preface   6
Photo Credits   7

Part One: A History of the Coal Industry in The Llynfi Valley

ONE	Introduction	11
TWO	The Geological Background	13
THREE	The Early Phase of Coal Mining 1770–1860	16
FOUR	The Beginning of Deep Mining 1860–1890	22
FIVE	The Victorian Township	30
SIX	North's Navigation Collieries (1889) Ltd	37
SEVEN	Elder's Navigation Collieries Ltd	48
EIGHT	The Hazards of Mining	54
NINE	Masters and Men: Industrial Disputes in the Llynfi Valley Coal Industry	63
TEN	The Types of Coal Produced in the Llynfi Valley	77
ELEVEN	The Decline of Coal 1924–1939	81
TWELVE	The End of Coal Mining	88

Part Two: The Collieries

Caedefaid Colliery   92
Caerau Colliery   93
Coegnant Colliery   98
Garth Colliery   106
Maesteg Deep Colliery   110
Oakwood Colliery   115
St John's Colliery   119
Other Collieries and Mine-Workings   127

Part Three: For Reference

For Reference   136
The Llynfi Valley Coal Industry: Sources of Information   155
Index   158

PREFACE

This study attempts to make a record of the development of the coal industry in the upper Llynfi Valley. Although primarily a local survey, as the district was a major exporter of high-quality fuel for many years and attracted the investment capital of 'global operators' such as Colonel John North and Sir Alfred Jones, there is some emphasis on the international events which, directly and indirectly, influenced the industrial development of the valley.

Wherever possible, contemporary documents and contemporary newspapers and journals have been used in the compilation of this history, although, due to lack of accessible primary materials, there are inevitable gaps in the record. As geology is the key element in any mining study, some emphasis has been placed on the geological background, hopefully in a way that is accessible to the general reader.

The study is divided into three parts: a chronological survey, an illustrated account of local collieries and mine-workings and a reference section with statistical material. Although the survey includes information which relates to the years after nationalisation in 1947, the bulk of the contemporary material consulted refers to the development of the coal industry up to the Depression years of the 1930s.

As the survey is based on contemporary materials it could not have been completed without the help of numerous individuals and the staffs of several libraries and archives. Particular thanks are due to Mr John Lyons, for his help and encouragement; Mr John Delaney of the Coal Authority, Mansfield; Professor Peter Davies and Mr J. Stokoe of the Liverpool Nautical Research Society, and the staff at the Bridgend Reference and Information Centre.

David Lewis,
October 2005

PICTURE CREDITS

The author would like to thank the following for permission to reproduce the photographs on the pages listed below:

Mr Bryan Davies: 73
The Glamorgan Record Office, (Crown Copyright material reproduced under Licence No.V2005000257 in this publication): 96 (lower), 97 (top), 100 (lower), 101 (top), 102(2), 103, 104, 112 (top), 121(3), 122(2), 123 (top), 124 (lower)
HMRS/Birmingham C&W Co. Collection: 120 (inset)
HMRS/Hurst Nelson Collection: 115 (inset)
HMRS/Gloucester C&W Co. Collection: 99 (inset)
Mr Bernard Ingram: 105 (lower), 125 (lower)
Leeds Museums and Galleries: 40
Mrs Iris Lewis: 125 (top)
Mr John Lyons: 19, 25, 51 (top), 89, 92, 94(2), 95(2), 97 (lower), 101(2), 105 (top), 108 (centre), 111(2), 113 (lower), 118 (top), 126(2)
National Library of Scotland: 51 (lower)
National Museums and Galleries of Wales: 106, 108 (lower), 109 (top), 116 (top), 124 (top)
Mr Ian Pope: 100 (centre)
Mr Paul Sharpe: 113 (top), 114(2)
Royal Commission on the Ancient and Historical Monuments of Wales (RCAHMW): 123 (lower)
University of Greenwich: 153 (top right)
University College, Swansea, The South Wales Coalfield Collection: 153 (lower)

PART ONE

A HISTORY OF THE COAL INDUSTRY IN THE LLYNFI VALLEY

CHAPTER ONE

INTRODUCTION

The development of the rich pocket of mineral wealth exposed in the upper Llynfi Valley, in the centre of the South Wales Coalfield, created a large community with a distinctive history. The natural resources of the district prompted the economic development of the Llynfi Valley in the nineteenth century and, such was the concentration of local mineral wealth, that a remarkable range of industrial activity developed in an area of just six square miles. There were two large ironworks in production during the years 1828 to 1885, a large tinplate works was in operation from 1869 to 1897, and one of the first zinc smelters in Wales produced spelter locally during the period 1831 to 1842. In addition, the collieries in a three-mile section of the valley from Garth to Caerau employed over 7,000 men during the heyday of the South Wales coal trade.

The mineral wealth inevitably attracted a range of investors to the district. In the early Victorian period, for example, when local coal mining was associated with iron making, the poet William Wordsworth was one of about ninety-five shareholders in the Cambrian Iron & Spelter Co., the first large enterprise to develop the mineral wealth of the district. Fellow investors included Sir Felix Booth, the wealthy gin distiller who sponsored the Ross expedition to the Arctic in the early 1830s, and Sir John Bowring, who was later governor of Hong Kong. Bowring, who had been a prime mover in the formation of the Anti-Corn Law League and introduced the florin 'decimal' coin in Britain, was heavily involved with the development of the Maesteg area in the 1840s and, for some years, the growing township was known as Bowrington. During the period 1890 to 1910 the rapid growth of the valley was prompted by the initiatives of two remarkable entrepreneurs: Colonel John North, the 'Nitrate King', and Sir Alfred Jones, the 'Napoleon of Commerce'.

With the development of industry came an influx of population that transformed the valley from an area of scattered farms to a large urban district and a major market centre by the early twentieth century. Initially the incomers were from adjoining parts of Glamorgan, and these were followed by migrant workers and their families from West and North Wales, Ireland and the West of England. The nineteenth-century township that emerged due to the development of the local coal and iron ore reserves retained its Welsh traditions and became a centre for religious nonconformity and eisteddfodau.

From the earliest years of its industrial development, the Llynfi Valley quickly established trading links with foreign markets. Initially, in the early 1830s, much of the pig iron produced at the Maesteg Ironworks was exported to France. In the mid-nineteenth century the large Llynfi Ironworks supplied regular shipments of wrought iron to customers in southern Italy, Turkey and Portugal, and large tonnages of wrought-iron rails were produced for buyers in, for example, Sweden, Germany and the United States. However, it was the development of the valley's coal resources that established the reputation of the district in the global marketplace. Because of the suitability of local coal resources for steam-raising, and the world-wide interests of Colonel North and Sir Alfred Jones, the Llynfi Valley played an important role in the booming South Wales coal trade during the years 1890 to 1924. For example, North opened up a significant market along the west coast of South America when he exported the first South Wales coal, from his Llynfi Valley collieries, to the Chilean nitrate works in the mid-1890s; Alfred Jones, with his connections in the shipping industry, ensured that coal from his local collieries was supplied to the major steamship lines.

As with all the South Wales Coalfield settlements, industrial development in the Llynfi Valley created dynamic communities with a strong emphasis on educational opportunity, religious, cultural and sporting activities. In the field of education, for example, Dr Philip Boswood Ballard (1865–1950), who was born and educated in Maesteg, became a divisional inspector of schools in the London area, and a leading pioneer of modern educational psychology. Arguably the most influential personality to emerge from the local mining community was George Jeffreys (1889–1972), a former collier from Nantyffyllon, who established the world-wide Elim Pentecostal Church in the early 1920s. Today there are over 500 Elim churches in Britain and more than 8,000 in forty-two countries world-wide. Christopher Williams (1873–1934), who was born and brought up in Maesteg, was a prominent portrait and landscape painter in the early twentieth century and Vernon Hartshorn (1872–1931), a local miners' leader, was the first former Welsh miner to become a cabinet minister.

Although the mining industry created energetic societies with strong community values, industrialisation brought costs as well as benefits. The hazards involved in the production of coal resulted in frequent deaths, serious injuries and long-term, disabling illness. Although conditions underground considerably improved after the Second World War, during the peak years of coal production in the Llynfi Valley, there was. on average, one fatal accident every seven weeks in the district.

Today the upper Llynfi Valley is predominantly a residential area with significant light industries. Twenty years after the closure of the last local colliery, with the scars of industrialisation rapidly disappearing, this survey attempts to make a record of the industry that helped create the community in the Llynfi district.

CHAPTER TWO

THE GEOLOGICAL BACKGROUND

The Llynfi Valley is one of the older mining areas in South Wales as coal from the district was relatively easy to mine at a time of limited mining technology. As much of the coal was on or near the surface, and production was linked with local iron making, the valley began its industrial development in the late 1820s, about forty years before the era of deep mining and the consequent rapid growth of the South Wales Coalfield.

As can be seen in the diagram below, the coal-bearing rocks of the Llynfi Valley are up-folded and reach the surface along the Maesteg anticline. The upper seams of the middle coal measures outcropped on the valley sides, and a number of the lower seams were exposed along the valley floor, around what later became the town centre of Maesteg. The diagram also shows the Moel Gilau fault which runs from Cwmfelin, along the south western side of the Llynfi Valley, to Bryn. The down throw of the fault is about 700 yards (650m), so the coal seams abruptly disappear to the south and west of the Moel Gilau fault and re-appear on the southern outcrop of the coalfield.

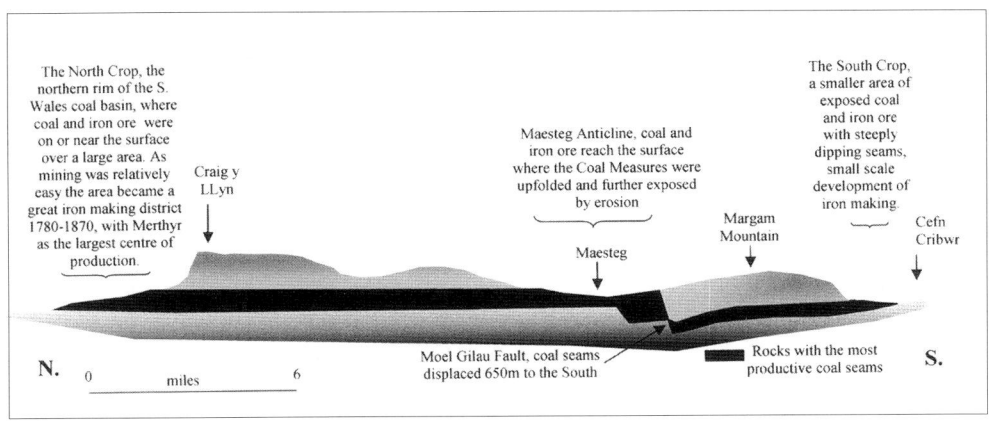

Simplified section across the South Wales Coalfield.

The diagram below gives some indication of the enormous coal wealth of the upper Llynfi Valley. At least twenty seams, suitable for a range of markets, have been worked in the valley between Garth and Caerau. The seams above the *Two Feet Nine* outcropped around the valley sides, especially on the eastern slopes. The coals were bituminous general-purpose fuels, and were extensively worked from levels in the earlier phase of mining before 1890. The seams from the *Two Feet Nine* to the *Caerau (Seven Feet),* together with bands of ironstone, were on or near the surface around the site of the present-day town centre of Maesteg, and some of the seams were cheaply mined from surface workings. The outcrops provided the raw materials for the first phase of iron making in the valley during the period 1828–43.

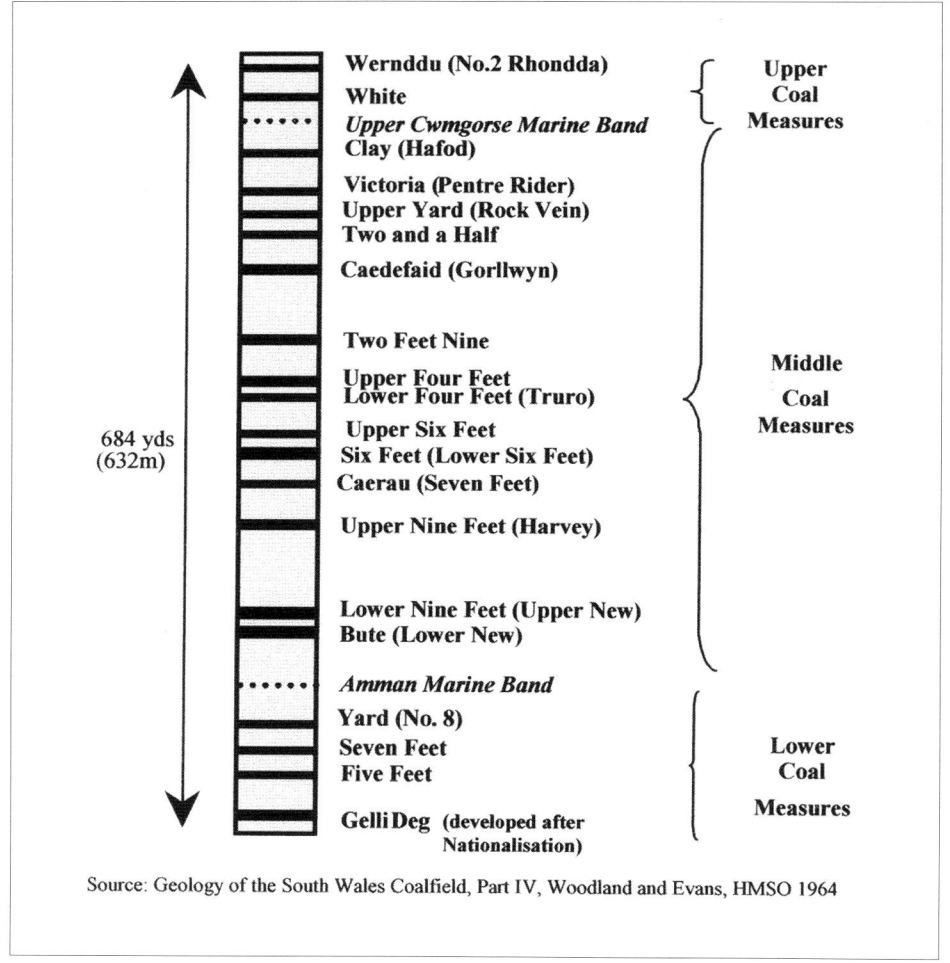

Major coal seams worked in the Upper Llynfi Valley (not to scale). An attempt has been made to standardise the names of the seams worked in the district by using the widely-applied 'Aberdare sequence' below the *Two Feet Nine*. Some of the alternative names used at North's collieries for those lower seams are included in brackets. The *Upper Four Feet* seam was sometimes referred to as the *Truro* but, generally, that name was applied to the *Lower Four Feet*.

Coal seams that outcropped (or were close to the surface) around the town centre of Maesteg (superimposed on a photograph of the town taken around 1947).

The coals from the *Two Feet Nine* to the *Bute* seams were fully exploited when deep mining developed on a large scale during the period 1895–1924. The seams generally dip steeply away from the centre of Maesteg; the *Two Feet Nine* for example, is close to the surface near Commercial Street, but was worked at 223 yards (206m) at Garth Colliery, a mile or so away.

The deeper seams also become more bituminous from north to south, so the highest grade steam coal occurs in the northern part of the valley and was mined at Caerau Colliery. The lowest major seam in the district, the *Gelli Deg*, was fully developed in the 1960s and 1970s.

CHAPTER THREE

THE EARLY PHASE OF COAL MINING 1770–1860

Although records of small-scale coal working from outcrops in the Llynfi Valley date back to the sixteenth century, the first reference to a limited form of commercial mining in the district dates from 1772. In that year Llewellyn David of Llwyni Farm entered into an agreement with John Bedford for the supply of coal to the ironworks the latter was planning at Cefn Cribwr, about eight miles away. Bedford's venture was not a success, but the original indenture drawn up between the two men allows a rare glimpse of coal production in the Llynfi Valley in the pre-industrial era. The document was transcribed in 1931 and published in the transactions of the Aberavon and Margam Historical Society for that year. In the indenture Llewellyn David states that, 'by long experience', he is able to produce up to thirty weys of coal per week from his workings on the Llwyni property, which was located about three-quarters of a mile to the north-east of the present-day town centre of Maesteg. In the same document a 'wey' is described as seven tons. From the indenture therefore, the workings at Llwyni in the early 1770s could produce up to 200 tons of coal per week. As part of the agreement with John Bedford, Llewellyn David stipulated that three months' notice should be given if more than fifty tons were required and one month's notice was required if between five and fifty tons were needed. Amounts up to five tons could be supplied on demand. Thus, from the indenture, it is evident that the coal at Llwyni was 'cut to order' by the farmer and not produced as part of a full-time mining operation. The price of Llewellyn David's coal, at the mine, was 16s per hundred sacks, and it was agreed that each 'sack or measure shall weigh at least two hundred weight when dry'. The fuel was expensive to transport as buyers had to rely on packhorses and farm carts to haul the coal from Llwyni. Haulage difficulties thus placed constraints on the development of Llynfi Valley coal, and it is probable that output figures did not increase significantly until communications were improved in the late 1820s.

In 1828, a horse railway was opened linking Garn-lwyd, which was about half a mile to the south-west of the farmhouse at Llwyni, to a coastal inlet at Porth Cawl fifteen miles away. A harbour and wharfage were constructed at the coastal site. By 1830 the railway had been extended to its northern terminus at Dyffryn Llynfi in the Coegnant district. Although initially developed as an outlet for the newly-opened Maesteg Ironworks, the railway, the Dyffryn Llynvi and Porth Cawl Railway (DLPR), also gave entrepreneurs the opportunity to supply local coal to a wider range of markets.

One of the first references to commercial mining on an industrial scale in the Llynfi Valley appeared as an advertisement in *The Cambrian* on 20 August 1830. The advertiser, David Jones at Coegnant Colliery Wharf, Porthcawl, gave notice that: 'Large Coal is for sale at 8*s* 6*d* per ton and Small Coal at 7*s* per ton'. The notice is of interest as it shows that trading outlets had been quickly set up after the completion of the DLPR, and the advertisement is also significant as it marks the beginning of the Coegnant district's 150-year association with commercial mining. That association ended in 1981 with the closure of another Coegnant Colliery, the deep mine sunk during 1881–3.

The Coegnant Colliery of 1830 was, typically, a small level on the lower slopes of the valley, east of the present-day community of Nantyffyllon. The *Caedefaid*, the *Two and a Half*, the *Upper Yard* and the *Victoria* seams outcropped in the area, and the level was driven into the hillside for a short distance to work one or more of those seams.

The coal resources of Coegnant Farm were also worked by James Hodgkins Allen of Neath in the 1830s. He took out a lease on the property in 1830 and set up a spelter works near the northern terminus of the DLPR, using imported zinc ores and local coal. Allen's works was one of the first zinc smelters in Wales, yet very little is known about the venture. It was probably in production from about 1832 to 1842, and, from a sale notice of 1844, there were seven zinc furnaces at the site. In the 1841 Census, twenty-four speltermen were listed in the Coegnant district, one of the largest concentrations in Glamorgan at that time. Almost all the speltermen lived in Toncwd Row, a newly-built, isolated terrace near the works. By tracing the birthplaces of the spelter workers on the 1851 census, we can see that the majority came to the Llynfi Valley from the Bristol district where spelter production was well-established. By 1851 many of the workers had left the local area for spelter works at Skewen and at Plasmarl, Swansea.

The easily accessible coking coal in the Coegnant district and the tramroad link to the coast presumably drew Allen to the upper Llynfi Valley in the first place. About twenty tons of coal, in the form of crushed coke, were used to produce one ton of zinc in the early 1830s so it was logical to locate a smelter near a source of cheaply-mined, high-quality coking coal. Allen employed about sixty workers at the Coegnant coal levels that supplied the works in the mid-1830s. Some coal was produced for sale as, according to the records of the DLPR during the period 1832–37, an annual average of 2,786 tons of coal was carried on the tramway from J.H. Allen's coal workings at Coegnant to the port at Porthcawl.

About a mile or so to the south of the Coegnant property, four of the best seams in South Wales were on (or near) the surface along the valley floor and along the lower slopes of the eastern side of the valley. The seams were the *Two Feet Nine*, the *Four Feet,* the *Six Feet* and the *Caerau* (*Seven Feet*) seams. The last three seams were probably cheaply worked from patches or open pits. Clay ironstone was also mined along with the coal and, in the 1830s, most of the output was used to supply the two blast furnaces at the Maesteg Ironworks.

Thus in the 1830s and for the ensuing two decades, when iron making was the dominant industry in the district, local coal was mined primarily as a blast furnace fuel. During the four years 1836 to 1839, for example, when the Maesteg Works was producing around 7,000 tons of pig iron per year, about 17,500 tons of coal were mined each year to supply its two furnaces. Some years later in 1860, a detailed report on the Maesteg Ironworks, which was compiled by the valuers and surveyors, Thomas Woodhouse and Samuel Dobson, allows a rare glimpse of local coal production in the mid-nineteenth century. According to the report, R.P. Lemon & Co., the owners of the works during the years 1852–60, produced coal from a large surface excavation known as the No.3 Patch, as well as from at least four coal levels and a 'deep' mine, all located within half a mile of the furnaces. A short distance to the east the company also owned a cluster of six coal and black-band ironstone levels at Blaen Cwmdu.

Woodhouse and Dobson estimated that the No.3 Patch could yield 3,000 tons of high-quality coal per year from the *Furnace Vein* (or *Six Feet* seam). It was also stated in their report that on the hillside above the furnaces, the *Caedefaid* seam was worked from the No.7 Level, above that the *Upper Yard* seam was mined from Level No.9, and higher still, the *Victoria* seam was worked from No.11 and No.12. The company also mined the high-quality coking coal of the *Six Feet* seam from their No.1 Pit. The pit, one of the first vertical shafts to be developed in the valley, is difficult to trace. It is possibly the mine marked as the 'Crown Pit' on R.H. Tiddeman's 1896 geological survey map of the Maesteg district. That pit adjoined the Maesteg Ironworks (or the Old Works) and probably consisted of two shafts sunk to a depth of 60 yards. According to the report, the No.1 Pit consisted of a winding engine, a pumping engine and an underground 'hauling engine', and the mine was 'capable of raising 200 tons a day'. During the period 1852–59, R.P. Lemon & Co. produced an average of 50,620 tons of coal per year with a production peak of 58,204 tons in 1858. The coal was used in the company's three blast furnaces; on average, two-and-a-quarter tons of coal were used to produce each ton of pig iron.

One of the investors in R.P. Lemon's Maesteg venture was Charles Sheppard, a young engineer originally from Bath. In the mid-1850s he decided to set up his own iron-making enterprise and opened a small ironworks at Cwmdu, about a mile to the east of the Maesteg furnaces. The Cwmdu Works was briefly in production with one furnace in blast from 1857 to 1859, and it seems that Sheppard sunk a small mine at Llwydarth in the late 1850s, presumably to supply his Cwmdu furnace. James Barrow, the Llynfi Valley colliery owner and mining engineer, writing in 1872, refers to a pit that was sunk by Charles Sheppard to the

'Yard coal'. Apart from Barrow's note there is little information about 'Sheppard's Pit' and it was not recorded in Tiddeman's geological survey of the valley in the late nineteenth century. However the shaft shown below, which was filled-in in 1995, was probably the one sunk by Sheppard. The pit was located near the present-day Hibernian Club, and the *Yard* seam (*Upper Yard* or *Rock Vein*) was close to the surface nearby at the north end of Llwydarth Road. From the photograph it was clearly a small-scale venture with a narrow, 7ft-diameter shaft.

After his unsuccessful ventures in the Llynfi Valley, Charles Sheppard established the firm of Sheppard & Sons, engineers, in Bridgend in 1862. In 1867 a report in the local press includes a note that a large steam engine at the Llynfi Ironworks had been built at Sheppard's Bridgend works. During the 1870s Sheppard's son, Oliver, joined the firm and for many years the enterprise specialised in the production of colliery machinery and coal-washery equipment.

In the late 1830s the 'New Works' was developed by the Cambrian Iron & Spelter Co. across the river to the west of the Maesteg furnaces. Although the new venture was a short distance from the Maesteg Ironworks, mining conditions were quite different. The Pen-y-Castell fault runs north–south along the valley, roughly following the line of the river Llynfi from Caerau to a point near the town centre of Maesteg. The 'down throw' of the fault is on the west side, so the *Six Feet* seam for example, which is very close to the surface near Plasnewydd School, is about 87 yards (80m) below the surface on the other side of the fault under Maesteg Park. As a result of the Pen-y-Castell fault and the dip of the strata, the best coking coal seams had to be worked from fairly deep pits at the New Works although the higher seams could still be mined from levels on the valley sides below Garnwen. Patch workings to the west of the river were not as extensive as the eastern side. The patches were mainly used for iron ore production.

Mine shaft at Llwydarth Road in 1995, probably Sheppard's Pit, sunk around 1856.

The first reference to one of the New Works' coal mines comes from the records of the Neath Abbey Iron Co. In 1840 that company supplied two steam engines for the 'Nant-y-Crynwith [Crynwydd] Colliery' of the Cambrian Iron & Spelter Co. It is likely that the Nant-y-Crynwydd Colliery was also known as the 'Office Level', a mine that was mentioned in correspondence in 1846 between the iron company and the Margam Estate. The Cambrian company also developed one or more of J.H. Allen's well-established levels in the Coegnant district during the early 1840s, probably on Tygwyn-bach Farm. Allen had been a prime mover in the formation of the new iron and spelter company, and his zinc smelter and its associated coking coal levels became part of the Cambrian property in 1838.

A rare report to the shareholders of the Cambrian Iron & Spelter Co., at the National Library of Wales, includes some references to coal production at the New Works during the first years of the venture. During the second half of 1838, shortly after the formation of the company, just 4,207 tons of coal were mined, about 700 tons a month. A year later, as more workings were opened up, the monthly output had risen to 4,115 tons. It was also noted that in September 1839 there were 28,409 tons of coal and coke stocked 'on the bank'. According to the report, the company kept large stocks of fuel on-site, as an 'insurance policy', to provide 'a wholesome check to the advantages which colliers and miners will sometimes endeavour to obtain, by strike for wages, when stock runs low'.

In 1845 the ambitious Llynvi Iron Co. bought the Cambrian property, and, in 1853, the enterprise was re-formed as the Llynvi Vale Iron Co. The Llynfi companies seem to have developed their coal resources during the early 1850s as a number of new levels were opened up and some of the first vertical shafts in the valley were sunk. Levels were opened on the slopes of Garnwen, near the ironworks, and the Nant-y-Crynwydd Colliery was probably developed as the 'Pwll Gwaith Newydd', or Gin Pit, that was recorded as working in the period 1850–75. The latter name could refer to a horse gin used for winding at the colliery, or the name could be the shortened form of 'Engine Pit'. The Gin Pit was sunk through the coking coal seams and iron ore 'pins' to the *Caerau (Seven Feet)* seam at about 100 yards. The colliery consisted of an up cast shaft and ventilation chimney on higher ground to the west of the blast furnaces, and an entrance adit, or 'horseway', probably at a lower level on the ironworks site. The pit was worked in conjunction with another of the iron company's collieries, the deeper Dyffryn Madoc Pit 500 yards to the north, which was eventually sunk to the *Upper Nine Feet (Harvey)* seam at 203 yards. A third pit, Blaenllynfi Colliery, was opened by the iron company, probably during the early 1850s. The mine was located near the present-day Square in Caerau and was sunk to the *Caedefaid* seam at 60 yards. In February 1858 the owners of the mine, the Llynvi Vale Iron Co., were prosecuted at the Bridgend Petty Sessions for a breach of colliery regulations. From the report of the case in the *Bridgend Chronicle*, there was a workforce of twenty-nine at the colliery, and the pit had been in production for at least three years.

Another ironworks, at Tondu, six miles to the south, was supplied with Llynfi Valley coal and black-band ironstone. Dafydd Morganwg, writing in the early

1870s, refers to a level at Tywith, Coegnant, which was opened in 1846 by Sir Robert Price, the owner of the Tondu Ironworks.

A fifth ironworks, the short-lived Garth Works, was opened in 1846 by Messrs Malins and Rawlinson, trading as the Patent Galvanized Iron Co. The works was supplied with black-band ironstone and coal from a number of levels on the west side of Garth Hill, and from a colliery with possibly the first vertical shaft in the valley. It is likely that the pit was sunk in the mid 1840s on the outcrop of the upper black-band on the hillside about 150 yards south-east of Caergymrig farmhouse. This was possibly the Coed-y-Garth Colliery, which was at the centre of a major industrial dispute in 1845. The colliery employed about sixty workers and was connected to the ironworks site by a 900-yard tramway. The Garth Works ceased production in the early 1850s and the mines associated with the venture probably closed at about the same time.

Some details of the working conditions in the Llynfi Valley coal levels during the earlier phase of mining are included in the Report of the Royal Commission: 'The Employment of Children and Young People in Mines and Manufactories'. The report was compiled in 1841 and published the following year. In his evidence to the commissioner, Charles Hampton, the manager of the Maesteg Ironworks, stated that his company's coal seams ranged from 18in to 12ft in thickness, and both 'carburetted hydrogen [methane] and carbonic acid gas [carbon dioxide]' were hazards. There had been explosions in the workings but no lives had been lost. From figures included in the report, about twenty children and young people were employed underground; eighteen were hauliers driving horse-drawn trams out of the levels, and there were two boys attending ventilation doors and flues. No females were employed underground and there were no children hauling trams (or 'drawing by the belt') in the coal levels.

At the New Works, H. Cooper, the clerk to the Cambrian Iron & Spelter Co., informed the commissioner that all the company's mines were entered by levels and the minimum height of the mainways in the mines was 5ft 6in. The thickness of the coal seams varied from 18in to 6ft. Cooper also stated that:

> …there are noxious gases existing in our mines occasionally but they are ventilated by fires when it exists. No explosion has taken place of any consequence within the last two years. One accident attended with loss of life has occurred within the last two years which was occasioned by the man's imprudence on not securing the roof as ordered.

As was the case in the mines supplying the Maesteg Works, coal was brought to the surface in horse-drawn trams and there were no children hauling with 'chain or girdle'. The commissioner, Rhys William Jones, noted that the proportion of women and children employed was considerably less in the Maesteg district than in the older iron-making centres of the north crop.

CHAPTER FOUR

THE BEGINNING OF DEEP MINING 1860–1890

At the end of the 1850s there were thus four small iron company pits in the Llynfi Valley: the Gin Pit, Dyffryn Madoc Colliery, Blaenllynfi Colliery and the Maesteg Works No.1 Pit, as well as Charles Sheppard's small-scale sinking at Llwydarth. There were also twenty or so levels of varying sizes, and a number of 'open-cast' workings called 'patches'. The 1860s would see the transformation of the coal industry in the district as the horse railway was replaced by a broad gauge, low-level track with locomotives, and demand for certain types of Welsh coal began to increase considerably.

The horse-drawn DLPR had been re-formed as the Llynvi Valley Railway (LVR) in 1847 and, although it had opened up the valley in the late 1820s, by the 1840s the horse railway was generally regarded as a constraint on the industrial development of the district. As it was a high-level railway, critics complained that it discouraged the development of collieries on the valley floor as entrepreneurs would have to construct expensive embankments and incline planes to connect any new mines to the tramway. In addition, the cost of transporting coal on the horse railway had always been relatively high. In 1844, for example, tramway transport costs were highlighted in a survey of the coal reserves of Troedyrhiw Farm in Cwmfelin. The survey included the estimated production costs if a colliery were to be sunk on the farm. The surveyor, Lionel Brough, estimated that the total cost of Troedyrhiw coal on the wharf at Porthcawl would be 6*s* per ton of which 2*s* would be the cost of cutting the coal and 2*s* 2*d* (36 per cent) would be the cost of transport along thirteen miles of tramway to the port. Harbour dues were estimated at 7*d* and other costs, including royalties and the costs of colliery engines and machinery, made up the remaining 1*s* 3*d*.

By the early 1850s the horse railway had become something of a liability. Tolls on the LVR were high, the harbour at Porthcawl was inadequate and extra costs were incurred if coal producers decided to use other ports via the South Wales Railway which had opened in 1850. The additional costs were incurred as coal had to be transferred to broad gauge wagons where the standard gauge tramway reached the main line at Stormy, the rail junction near Pyle. Due to the high transport costs, Llynfi Valley coal producers found it difficult to compete in the sale-coal trade away from the local area. Producers in other localities, with lower transport costs, could sell more successfully at the ports of Cardiff, Briton Ferry and Swansea. Because of the transport difficulties, the report by Woodhouse and Dobson in 1860, referred to in the previous chapter, recommended that only 20,000 tons of coal (about 28 per cent of total output) should be produced for sale, 'along the Line of Railway... with occasional cargoes at all the ports'.

The situation began to change when the Llynvi Valley Railway was re-routed along the valley as a steam-hauled, low-level, broad gauge line; it opened for mineral traffic in 1861. The railway came too late for the owners of the Maesteg Works. Due to the 'pecuniary difficulties' of R.P. Lemon & Co., the works closed in 1860 and the furnaces were blown out. There is no evidence to suggest that they were ever in production again.

The ambitious firm of John Brogden & Sons had established a foothold in the valley in the late 1850s and, with the opening of the railway, sought to develop its coal mining operations in the Llynfi district. Alexander Brogden, one of the four sons, had once described the Llynfi and Ogmore Valleys as 'the best maiden coalfield in England!' and his company soon began to open coal workings on quite a large scale in the area. The founder of the firm, John Brogden, had been a successful railway contractor and iron mine owner in the north of England before he bought the Tondu Ironworks and its mineral estate in about 1854. During the late 1850s the Brogdens enlarged existing coal and black-band workings at Tywith, they opened up a level on the hillside above the Maesteg furnaces (probably the Scwd Level), and developed two levels at Cwmdu, one of which was previously owned by R.P. Lemon & Co. In 1864 the Brogdens sunk the Garth Pit to supply their two blast furnaces at Tondu and, more significantly, to supply the growing market for sale-coal. The colliery was the first of a generation of larger, deeper mines in the valley and was initially sunk to the *Caedefaid* seam at 136 yards (126m). Two seams above the *Caedefaid*, the *Two and a Half* at 112 yards and the *Victoria* at 58 yards, were worked from landing stages on the shaft.

The other large industrial enterprise in the district, the Llynvi Vale Iron Co. at the New Works, also looked to its coal resources with the coming of the railway. In 1862 the company bought the Maesteg Ironworks which had remained idle after the demise of R.P. Lemon & Co. two years earlier. The coal and ironstone workings were re-opened and the coke ovens were brought into operation at the Old Works site.

When the Maesteg Works was put up for sale in 1860, the valuers and surveyors, Woodhouse and Dobson, noted that the existing coal workings were 'not satisfactory'. Some of the workings were 'standing at faults', and the underground and surface roads were 'defective in construction and badly arranged'. They recommended that a 'winning should be sunk upon Cwrt-y-mwnws [Farm]', and that 'the whole system of transit should be rearranged'. In addition they suggested that rails should be 'substituted in all cases for tramplates, and all the trams altered to suit'. It was estimated that the improvements would cost £15,000, a considerable addition to the selling price of £35,500. The significant cost of upgrading the coal workings could explain why the works remained without a buyer from 1860 to 1862. The eventual purchaser, the Llynvi Vale Iron Co., had sufficient capital to carry out the improvements suggested by Woodhouse and Dobson. For example, the 'winning' at Cwrt y Mwnws Farm mentioned above, was probably carried through as Moffatt's Level, which was opened up in the late 1860s.

In October 1867 the scale of coal-working on the valley sides increased considerably with the redevelopment of the Caedefaid Colliery (or No.9 Level) by the Llynfi Vale venture, then trading as the Llynvi Coal & Iron Co. Ltd. The mine was driven into the hillside for over a mile to work the *Caedefaid* and *Victoria* seams as well as black-band ironstone. The coal was worked via a 'cross-measure drift' 8ft wide and 6½ft high, which was over 1,400 yards long. Initially ventilated by a furnace, the mine was probably the first in the valley to be fan-ventilated when a 24ft-diameter Waddle fan was installed soon after opening.

At about the same time, the company redeveloped the Blaenllynfi Pit. The redevelopment was evidently not a success as the pit was marked as an abandoned mine on the first edition of the 25in Ordnance Survey map, which was based on a survey of 1876. As mentioned above, Moffatt's Level was opened up on the hillside near the No.9 Colliery in the late 1860s. George Moffatt was the chairman of the Llynvi Coal & Iron Co. Ltd from 1866 to 1872. By 1875 Moffatt's Level, also known as Moffatt's Slip and Cwrt y Mwnws Colliery, was listed as Maesteg Deep Colliery.

As well as the two large companies operating in the district, independent entrepreneurs also became involved in the development of the coal resources of the Llynfi Valley. In 1869 the first coal was raised from the Oakwood Colliery owned by William Davis. Davis was born in Merthyr in 1821 and, in the 1851 census, he was listed as a colliery agent in the Aberdare district. By the mid-1860s he was living in Bridgend and, in partnership with his brother, Charles Price Davis, he began sinking the Oakwood Pit in 1868. The sinkers 'struck' the *Four Foot* seam in April 1869 and the colliery was in production by the end of the year. The mine was known locally as 'Davis's Pit' throughout its working life. Two shafts were sunk to a depth of 180 yards (166m) on the site of a small level, probably owned by Charles Sheppard, which had worked the *Caedefaid* seam. Initially the colliery worked the *Upper Four Feet* seam at 157 yards, the *Lower Four Feet* at 170 yards and the *Six Feet* seam.

Another colliery was developed near Davis's Pit in the early 1870s, although it is difficult to be precise about its origins and its development. On the first edition of the local Ordnance Survey map, which was based on a survey of 1875–6, a 'Maesteg Merthyr Pit' is shown adjoining the east side of Llwydarth Road about 300 yards to the south of Davis's Oakwood Colliery, close to the southern end of the line of Davis's bee-hive coke ovens. On the next edition of the map, in 1899, the site is marked as an abandoned mine. On a later edition of the Ordnance Survey map,

The entrance to Caedefaid Colliery (No.9 Level) in 1985. It was the largest of a number of levels that were opened up on the eastern slopes of the Llynfi Valley, and up to 400 workers would have passed through this arched portal on a daily basis during the late nineteenth century.

which was based on a revision of 1914, the pit is not marked but Davis's Oakwood Pit is named as 'Maesteg Merthyr Colliery'. Surprisingly, Tiddeman's very detailed geological survey map of the valley drawn up in 1896 makes no reference to the pit alongside Llwydarth Road.

From the limited amount of evidence available it is possible to suggest an explanation for the two 'Maesteg Merthyr' mines. In 1873, just four years after the opening of the Oakwood mine, William Davis attempted to sell his colliery enterprise to a newly formed joint stock company. From the company's file at the Public Record Office, the new venture, Davis's Merthyr Colliery Co. Ltd, was floated in October 1873 with a capital of £160,000 in £10 shares. For legal reasons there was an objection to the unqualified use of the name 'Merthyr' in the title, so the enterprise was re-named Davis's Maesteg Merthyr Colliery Co. Ltd in January 1874. A small group of London speculators led by George Batters, a share dealer, were the major investors in the new venture. However, the attempt at flotation seems to have failed and the Davis family retained the ownership of the company until the early 1880s. It is possible that the Maesteg Merthyr Pit alongside Llwydarth Road was developed as an extension of Davis's existing mine during the optimistic period when he floated the new company in 1873.

From the first edition of the Ordnance Survey map the Llwydarth Pit was quite a substantial colliery with a single shaft, surface buildings and screens above sidings that were adjacent to the Maesteg–Bridgend railway line. It could have been a development of previous workings started by Charles Sheppard, or an enlargement of the Oakwood Pumping Pit which was marked in the Llwydarth district on sections drawn up in the early 1870s by the local mining engineer, James Barrow. Whatever its origins, the pit alongside Llwydarth Road was a short-lived venture and seems to have ceased production during the trade depression of the late 1870s. On later maps and colliery lists, the 'Maesteg Merthyr' company name was thus often used to identify the mine known locally as 'Davis's Pit' or 'Oakwood Colliery'.

As the coal industry developed, there was an influx of workers and a consequent shortage of accommodation. Such was the demand for housing that the owners of the Oakwood mine sought permission from the Cwmdu Board of Health to build thirty-six wooden houses for the workforce. The board agreed provided that certain fire-proofing measures were employed in their construction. The temporary dwellings were probably built on the appropriately named Wood Street, a short distance from the mine. Thirty-six houses, in six blocks of six dwellings, are shown on the first large-scale Ordnance Survey map of the district in 1884. The site had been cleared by the time of the 1899 edition of the Ordnance Survey map. The 1919 edition shows the present-day housing in Wood Street.

In 1872 the pattern of colliery ownership in the Llynfi Valley was transformed when eight of the nine major mines in the district came into the possession of a newly created venture, the Llynvi, Tondu & Ogmore Coal & Iron Co. Ltd. The new company, which was registered in May 1872, was an amalgamation of the properties of John Brogden & Sons and the Llynvi Coal & Iron Co. Ltd. The merging of the two companies was probably inevitable as in 1870 an expensive lawsuit resulted when the underground workings of one company encroached on the coal reserves of the other. In the High Court the Llynfi company argued that, in 1867, miners at the Tywith Colliery of Brogden & Sons had crossed the boundary of the adjoining workings of the Llynfi enterprise and had illegally extracted large quantities of coal from the *Caedefaid* seam of the latter company. The vice-chancellor, Sir James Bacon, ruled in favour of the Llynvi Coal & Iron Co. and the Brogdens had to pay a large amount in compensation or face an expensive appeal. Some months later, in December 1871, the problem seems to have been resolved when Brogden & Sons merged with the Llynfi company before both ventures became part of the new Llynvi, Tondu & Ogmore Coal & Iron Co. Ltd. The new enterprise was the result of an initiative by the Brogden family; Alexander and Henry Brogden were the major shareholders and Alexander Brogden was the chairman of the new venture. After the merger, James Barrow, the Brogdens' mineral agent, managed all the mining properties of the new company.

During the early 1870s the new company wanted to gain access to the considerable reserves of prime steam coal under Mynydd Caerau, to the north of their own mineral estate. By the mid-1870s negotiations were under way with the various landowners of the Mynydd Caerau property so that agreements could be drawn up. Because maps were inadequate and boundaries imprecise, disputes often arose during the drafting of leases. One of James Barrow's letters, written in January 1875, survives among the Gnoll Papers at the West Glamorgan Record Office; it gives some indication of the rather 'informal' way that agreements were often made. At the request of the mining engineer, T. Forster-Brown, Barrow had to confirm a boundary on the land of G. Jenkins esq. of Gelli Farm near Cymer Afan, the master of the famous Gelli Hunt. He replied:

> What with my being away for a fortnight & having called to see Mr. Jenkins 3 times & could not meet him I have been unable to reply to your favour & instruction of the 7th Ultimo. I now beg to say that I rode up to Gelli again this morning & found Mr. Jenkins out hunting again. I rode after him a short distance & told him about the mountain property & referred to the plan on which he described his property at my house some time back. I then produced the enclosed plan (tracing) and he looked and examined it carefully & said it represents the line we walked over very well… I then and there drew a pencil line according to his instructions & he agreed that such a line represents his boundary… Having got this and the hounds getting further away I did not detain him any further…

Unfortunately for James Barrow, his coal and iron company would never develop the Mynydd Caerau district. Although there was great optimism at the time of the launch of the enterprise in 1872, it was in financial difficulties within four years of its formation. Profits began to fall after the company's employees joined a major strike in South Wales that began on 28 December 1872. The dispute proved costly for the Llynvi, Tondu & Ogmore Coal & Iron Co. and, after seven weeks, the directors brought the strike to an end in the district by settling independently with their miners and ironworkers. In the other iron-making districts of South Wales the dispute continued for another four weeks before ending in the middle of March 1873. In addition to the losses incurred by the strike, the mid-1870s proved to be disastrous years for the Llynfi company, and the South Wales iron industry generally, because of changing conditions in the iron trade. Annual losses increased as iron prices fell due to competition from foreign producers of cheaper wrought iron, and the growing importance of low cost mass-produced Bessemer steel.

Welsh merchant bar iron, which sold at £13 a ton in 1873, was selling at £5 2s 6d in 1877. With such low prices the loss-making coal and iron company sought significant wage reductions in December 1877 in a desperate attempt to make production costs more competitive. Before the question of wage reduction developed into a major dispute, the Llynvi, Tondu & Ogmore Coal & Iron Co. went into voluntary liquidation. The complex reasons that led up to that decision were explained in a company circular of 22 January 1878 which was reproduced three days later in the columns of the *Central Glamorgan Gazette*.

Because of losses of markets, low prices for iron and relatively high production costs, the firm was unable to make interest payments to its debenture holders. This situation had become apparent in October 1877 and, at that time, the majority of the holders opted to 'defer requiring payment for their principal and interest for twelve months' in an attempt to ease the company's financial problems. However, in December 1877, one major debenture holder decided not to renew his bond, thus making a demand on the company for about £43,000, the value of his debenture holding. In the trade depression of the late 1870s such a payment would have pushed the company into bankruptcy with disastrous consequences for the debenture holders. As a result of the threat to withdraw the bond for £43,000, the directors, 'after much consideration, and only under the pressure which the long-continued depression in the iron and coal trade has put upon the finances of the company, considered it would be wise to put the company into liquidation, with a view to financial rearrangement'. On 31 January 1878 a meeting was convened for the debenture holders, ironically at the Terminus Hotel, Cannon Street, London, and it was resolved that the company should be wound up voluntarily. After surviving a number of slumps over the previous thirty years, the Llynfi Works joined the growing list of South Wales ironworks that ceased large-scale production in the late 1870s.

The key bond-holder who was not prepared to renew his company debentures and who thus precipitated the move towards voluntary liquidation, was not named in the company statement but, from the limited amount of evidence available, it was probably George Moffatt, the former chairman of the Llynvi Coal & Iron Co. The press report refers to the bond-holder as 'one of the founders of the old Llynvi company'. In January 1878 Moffatt was the only surviving major investor, as the other key shareholder, Colonel Cavan, had died in 1870. Less than a month after the vote for voluntary liquidation, George Moffatt died at the Imperial Hotel, Torquay, at the age of seventy-two.

As a result of the general trade depression during the late 1870s and the trading difficulties of the Llynvi, Tondu & Ogmore Coal & Iron Co., the Llynfi Valley experienced levels of unemployment, poverty and distress on a scale that would not be repeated until the Depression years of the 1930s. Large numbers of workers and their families left the area, and future prospects seemed bleak. The Gin Pit had ceased production in 1875 and, in May 1878, the Dyffryn Madoc Pit was closed with the loss of 400 jobs. Another major colliery, the Garth Pit, was probably closed from 1878 to 1882 as the mine was not listed in the government's Mineral Statistics for those years.

As well as the problem of unemployment due to colliery closures, the wages of those in work were low and payments were irregular. For example, the colliers who lost their jobs when the Dyffryn Madoc Pit closed had not been paid for over ten weeks. In an attempt to alleviate the growing problem of poverty, a public meeting was called on 11 January 1878 and the Maesteg Distress Relief Committee was formed. In the same meeting it was decided to divide the valley into twelve districts and two persons were appointed for each district in order to evaluate levels of need in their areas. Each district would receive 30*s* to deal with immediate problems. A report of the activities of the Relief Committee in the *Central Glamorgan Gazette* for the period 21 January to 6 May 1878, gives some impression of conditions in the Llynfi Valley at that time. The soup kitchens opened by the committee supplied a daily average of 500 people with one pint of soup and 1lb of bread each for five weeks, 250 pairs of wooden clogs were distributed and, during the fifteen-week period covered by the report, '1,469 relief notes were issued to assist 5,876 persons or an average of 392 persons per week'.

In 1880, however, there were some grounds for optimism as the receiver appointed after the voluntary liquidation of the Llynvi, Tondu & Ogmore enterprise, John Joseph Smith, the company secretary, re-formed the venture as the Llynvi & Tondu Co. The new company, with limited resources, kept one furnace in blast at the Llynfi Works and, realising the potential of the Mynydd Caerau area for steam coal, the directors decided to open a new deep mine at Coegnant. Sinking commenced in October 1881, and two shafts, the North and South Pits, which were initially sunk to the *Caerau (Seven Feet)* seam at 150 yards (162m), were completed by June 1883. A year after the opening of Coegnant, the Garnwen, Tygwyn-bach, Tywith and Cwmdu levels ceased production, although Cwmdu and Tygwyn-bach were later re-opened as 'small mines'. The latter colliery employed about forty workers in the 1890s; the level was worked by the Maesteg Colliery Co. until it was finally abandoned in about 1907.

When the receiver, J.J. Smith, established the Llynvi and Tondu Co. in 1880, he retained all the old Llynfi company's mines in the valley except for Garth Colliery, which was sold off, probably in the same year. The mine was probably closed in the late 1870s and early 1880s and was re-opened in 1882 by the new owner, James Humby, an entrepreneur from Bath. Humby's Garth mine was managed by the local mining engineer, James Barrow. Initially, the *Caedefaid* seam was worked, then the pit was deepened to reach the *Six Feet* seam at 250 yards (231m).

During the mid-1880s the history of the Garth Pit is far from clear. A new venture, Garth Merthyr Steam Navigation Collieries Ltd, was floated in February 1883 with a board of directors that included General Addison of Merton, Suffolk, Thomas Saunders, a director of the Lake Superior Copper Co., and John Walker, a director of the Abbotsbury Railway Co. in Dorset. Walker and Humby were fellow directors of the Abbotsbury Railway, and it seems that James Humby had planned to sell Garth Colliery to the new company. Although the company name was adopted, the flotation was not a success as the colliery remained unsold and Humby was in financial difficulties by 1885. James Barrow then seems to have guided the fortunes of the mine until he joined a new partnership which took over the pit in 1887. Barrow's other partners were John and Richard Cory of Cardiff and Ebenezer Lewis of Newport.

Barrow and Lewis also became the joint owners of Oakwood Colliery, probably in the early 1880s. During that decade the mine seems to have traded quite successfully using the 'Davis' Maesteg Merthyr' brand name. In 1888 for example, price lists prepared for a Spanish customer by the colliery's Cardiff agents, Fry, Holman & Fry, indicate that 'Davis Maesteg Merthyr' steam coal and 'Davis Patent Coke' had international reputations in the markets for steamship bunkers and foundry work respectively.

CHAPTER FIVE

THE VICTORIAN TOWNSHIP

With the development of industry in the Llynfi Valley during the nineteenth century came the very slow process of change that gradually improved the living and working conditions of the local population. By the early 1840s, in little over a decade, a large part of the valley had been transformed from an area of scattered farms into an industrial district with a growing township of about 4,000 people. With such rapid growth there were already problems to be addressed. Public health, law and order, truck and the payment of wages, soon became issues which created tensions in the new township.

When the first ironworks opened in 1828, apart from the lifeline of the horse-railway, there was no basic framework around which to build a community. There were no shops and services, little or no housing and no system of local administration. By the end of the century Maesteg and district was a flourishing industrial and commercial centre administered by its own Urban District Council. However, the process of change would be tentative and slow.

One of the first contentious issues that faced the growing community was the problem of the truck system and the company shop, a major theme in the history of the Llynfi Valley from 1828 until truck was abandoned in 1869. Industrialists in the early nineteenth century often favoured a truck system based on wage-payment in the form of cheques or tokens which had to be used in their company shop. Although after 1831 truck was illegal, in reality it prevailed as a convenient, common practice, especially in the new industrial districts.

From the point of view of the iron companies, truck was obviously a good thing; it was of great importance in new settlements as it ensured that the workforce was fed and clothed in areas where there were, initially, no shops and services. Truck also enabled the employers to control and manipulate the workers by limiting their access to cash and by compelling them to rely on their stores for day-to-day necessities. Above all, the key element was profit; the revenue from the Maesteg Works' shop for example, made up about 20 per cent of the iron company's profits in the 1830s.

From the workers' point of view truck did, initially, provide the opportunity to acquire food and clothing in newly settled areas. However, as industrial communities developed, it was soon generally regarded as a burden as the system ensured that many aspects of a workman's life were completely controlled by the company. The miners and ironworkers had no choice but to spend their earnings at the company store, and faced dismissal and destitution if they challenged the system in any way.

A third party involved in the truck controversy consisted of a group of enterprising individuals who wished to break the company trading monopoly in the valley and set up their own shops. This group, especially in the 1850s, often took the lead and prompted anti-truck initiatives in the Maesteg district.

The history of truck in the Llynfi Valley began in the early 1830s when the Maesteg Co. built a shop for their miners and ironworkers at the bottom of present-day Garn Road. Then, in 1839, the Cambrian Iron & Spelter Co. built a large store for the workforce at the north end of their new ironworks. At about the same time, another company shop was opened for the colliers and spelter workers of the Coegnant district. In 1843 the situation changed dramatically when Dr John Bowring MP, then the leading partner in the Cambrian company, abandoned the truck system at his works and paid the workers in cash on a weekly basis. Although there is some evidence that Bowring favoured a company store in principle, he was forced to abandon an (illegal) truck system in Maesteg because of pressure from opponents in the House of Commons. He did however lease the store to a local trader as an independent venture to 'ensure a supply at all events' for his workers. As a result of the reforms of Dr Bowring, there was a cash-based local economy for the first time, and significant numbers of shops opened up in the township.

Sir John Bowring (1792–1872), writer and diplomat, Governor of Hong Kong 1854–59. During his involvement with the Maesteg iron industry in the 1840s, John Bowring ended the truck system at the Llynfi Works (for a time at least), and generally improved the living conditions of his workforce.

Ten years after Bowring had introduced cash wages and a 'free market' for his workers, his successor at the iron company, Alexander Macgregor, decided to end the weekly cash payments and re-introduce truck. His arguments for change reflected the 'traditional' pro-truck attitudes of the time and were included in his evidence to a Parliamentary Select Committee on the Payment of Wages in July 1854. Macgregor was concerned that heavy drinking on the weekly pay-days was the cause of the widespread absenteeism the next day which limited the production of coal and iron. He was also of the opinion that, by re-introducing truck, housewives could manage more effectively, as they had more control over family incomes when payment was in the form of company cheques. Above all, he was confident that the store would yield a profit of 10 per cent for his company and thus safeguard the livelihoods of the workforce during trade depressions.

Although the reintroduction of truck prompted the formation of an anti-truck association in Maesteg and was the cause of an unsuccessful ten-week strike in protest at the change, the community reluctantly accepted Macgregor's reforms. As a result, the company shop, together with a system of monthly pay cheques, flourished for another sixteen years. The worst aspect of truck was the coercion employed by the coal and iron companies to suppress any challenge to what was an illegal method of trading. It was only through coercion and fear that the system survived, as workers would not risk dismissal by openly criticising or challenging their employers.

For three decades after 1830 the Maesteg company shop at Garnlwyd flourished and yielded substantial profits for the companies operating the ironworks and its associated collieries. When the Maesteg Works was bought by the Llynvi Vale Iron Co. in 1862 the shop was then operated in conjunction with the main Llynfi Ironworks' store and the other company shop in the Spelter (Coegnant) district. During the 1860s thus, this 'Llynfi group' of stores ensured a trading monopoly in the valley for the proprietors of the Llynfi Works.

The Llynfi Valley truck system was finally abandoned in 1869 as the result of a legal challenge to the Llynfi company. The case, *Thomas Pillar* v. *The Llynvi Coal & Iron Co. Ltd* was heard at Bristol Spring Assizes. Thomas Pillar, a Maesteg tinsmith who worked part-time for the Llynfi company, courageously challenged the legality of the payment methods employed in the valley. During the hearing the details of truck in Maesteg were fully described. The management of the company shop had been taken over by a Mr Brittan in 1866 and the payment cheques of the Llynfi company were issued to the workforce at intervals of up to nine weeks, with 'intermediate draws' if required. If a cheque for £1 was presented at the company shop, it was exchanged for 16s-worth of goods and 4s were given in change. When Pillar challenged this system of payment, his Counsel called George Parker Hubbuck, a Monmouthshire JP, as a key witness. Hubbuck had been the managing director at the Llynfi Works for ten months during 1867 and his evidence convinced the court that the workers were compelled to use their cheques at the company shop in contravention of the Truck Act of 1831. However, before judgement was passed, the company wisely abandoned truck for their workers and the company shops were closed in June 1869. The end of truck allowed the development of other shops in the valley and prompted the beginning of a long campaign to open a central market in Maesteg.

Although truck ended in the valley after the prosecution brought by Thomas Pillar, the system of wage-payments in the Maesteg district was still far from a recognisable modern pattern. In fact the Llynfi Valley was one of the last areas in Britain to introduce the payment of cash wages on a weekly basis. The details of the payment methods employed in the valley, after the ending of truck, were given by James Colquhoun, manager of the Llynfi Works, and John J. Smith, the company secretary, in their evidence to government commissioners collecting information about the truck system in South Wales at the end of 1870.

At that time most of the colliers in the Llynfi Valley were employed by the Llynvi Coal & Iron Co. Ltd. They were paid in cash just six times a year: there were two pays at eight-week intervals and four at nine. Every fortnight, 'intermediate draws' were available for colliers and ironworkers who required payment at shorter intervals. At the time of the intermediate draws, 'Certificates of Earnings', which were negotiable in local shops, were issued to the workforce. The wording on one example of a certificate was quoted in evidence from Colquhoun: 'Llynvi Collieries and Ironworks, No.551. The person above named is entitled to 15*s*, which will be due and payable to him on account of wages, in coin, at the Company's pay, 5th November next'. The certificates were exchanged for goods at local shops and the traders cashed them at the works' office at the time of the next pay. On pay-day the value of the used certificates was deducted from the worker's earnings. About 27 per cent of the company's annual wage bill of £90,000 was paid out to local traders with certificates.

Colquhoun informed the commissioners that there were thirty-seven grocers and drapers in the valley, thirty-one other shops and fifty-nine public houses. The most important shops in the township were the former company stores then leased by a Mr Hyde. The main building was adjacent to the Llynfi Ironworks, and Hyde also operated shops at Garnlwyd, Nantyffyllon and Bridgend Road. J.J. Smith informed the commissioners that Hyde leased 'very capacious premises…under the company'; he employed eight counter assistants at the Llynfi Works' store, which also included a large bakery and a butcher's shop. The building had living accommodation for up to twenty assistants. According to company records for the most recent pay on 5 November 1870, £3,876 had been paid out to traders with certificates, of which just £289 (7½ per cent) was paid to publicans. In the previous pay, 38 per cent of the £4,500 paid to traders with certificates accrued to Mr Hyde.

Many of the arguments that had previously been put forward in support of truck and company shops were also referred to by Colquhoun and Smith when they defended the company policy of 'long pays' and certificates. According to James Colquhoun, drunkenness and the consequent absenteeism after pay-day were major problems for the company. With just six pay-days per year the problem could be contained. The works' manager was convinced that the system of certificates ensured that: 'the men worked more steadily, the wives obtained their husband's certificates to take to any place they chose, and the whole family was better cared for'.

Law and order was also an issue in the valley especially during the years of industrial depression in the early 1840s. A key feature of life in the new township was the absence of the 'ruling class' of local landowners who usually administered justice and influenced local affairs in the well-established settlements in South Wales. The initiatives that had created the new industries in the Llynfi Valley were generally undertaken by 'absentee entrepreneurs' who lived outside the district and delegated the operation of their collieries and ironworks to resident directors or works' managers. There was one exception, W.H. Buckland of the Maesteg Works, who lived locally at Plasnewydd House for much of the 1830s and during the 1850s. However, other South Wales-based investors lived outside the local district. For example, Robert Smith who was the senior partner at the Maesteg Works from 1835 to 1840, lived at Craigafan in Margam, and James Bicheno, a magistrate and an investor in the Maesteg Works during the 1830s, lived at Ty-Maen, South Cornelly. The wealthy entrepreneurs who funded the Llynfi Works for nearly thirty years were almost all London-based.

Although the resident works managers at the ironworks would later play active roles in the local community, it was left to the vicar of Llangynwyd, the Revd William Pendrill Llewellyn, to provide the much-needed leadership, stability and continuity required in a new township. The Revd Llewellyn had charge of the parish for fifty years (1841–91) and, especially in the early years, he played a key role in the development of the valley. During a difficult period in the South Wales iron-making districts, in the early 1840s, the Revd Llewellyn appealed to the Lord Lieutenant of Glamorgan (the Marquess of Bute) and the Home Secretary regarding the need for constables and a 'lock-up' to maintain public order in the Llynfi Valley. As a general trade depression, and a consequent breakdown of law and order, was affecting many industrial areas in the county, it seems that the authorities decided that the difficulties outlined by the vicar were not sufficiently serious to merit any special treatment.

However by 1846, after the formation of the Glamorgan Constabulary, one constable had been allocated to the Maesteg district. This did not satisfy Pendrill Llewellyn who informed the Marquess of Bute that unless there were more police constables and a suitable lock-up in the valley, another trade depression like that of 1841–2 would result in a complete breakdown of law and order in Maesteg. His letters to the marquess, in the Bute Collection at the National Library of Wales, give an insight into local conditions in the mid-1840s. In a letter dated 2 December 1846, the vicar informed the marquess that the single constable employed in the valley was insufficient for an isolated area with 'large numbers of violent individuals'. He also complained that the Llynvi Iron Co., which paid most of the local rates, was not prepared to pay more for extra police. The marquess was also informed that: 'if our one policeman takes those reprobates to their homes, as soon as his back is turned, they appear in the streets more furious than ever'. The vicar was also concerned that Caerphilly in the Newbridge district had obtained a lock-up and accommodation for a police constable, yet Maesteg, with seven times the population of Caerphilly, had no such facilities.

As well as addressing the problem of law and order, the long-serving vicar became involved, almost reluctantly, with the newly-formed Cwmdu Board of Health in 1858. The board was only the third to be established in the industrial areas of Glamorgan (after Merthyr Tydfil and Aberdare), and this was a measure of the growing importance of the Maesteg district in the county. The setting up of the board was the result of a petition of December 1857 and a survey by the General Board of Health in March 1858. The petition was presented by Dr James Lewis, the progressive local physician who would later establish The Rest at Porthcawl, and the survey was carried out by William Ranger, a government inspector.

Ranger's report included an assessment of the housing stock in the Maesteg district in 1858. Of the 594 dwellings surveyed, 130 (about 22 per cent) were 'back-to-back' houses which were sub-standard even for the mid-Victorian period. There seems to have been a marked difference between the hastily constructed housing around the Maesteg Works and the more substantial rows and streets built by the owners of the Llynfi Works. The latter company had built almost 300 houses for the workforce by the mid-1850s, compared with the seventeen cottages provided by the owners of the Maesteg Works. Much of the housing stock around the Maesteg Works had thus been hastily built by speculators and was cleared during the late Victorian period. In addition to housing quality, Ranger's report also highlighted the problems of water supply, sewerage and refuse disposal in the township, issues that were among the first to be addressed by the new Board of Health.

Typically, although Pendrill Llewellyn was not convinced of the necessity of a Board of Health in the valley, the vicar directed the fortunes of the board during its early years, almost by default. Although W.H. Buckland of Plasnewydd House, the resident director at the Maesteg Ironworks, was elected the first chairman of the Cwmdu Board of Health, he only attended six meetings out of about thirty-five during the board's first year. As a result of Buckland's poor attendance record, Pendrill Llewellyn chaired almost all the meetings in that first year. During that early period the drainage of Bowrington Street (present day Commercial Street) was a priority, and the board also introduced a new series of regulations in an attempt to improve public health in the district. For example, all new housing and extensions had to be approved by the Board of Health, and lodging houses were licensed for the first time. The initiatives of the board marked the beginning of a slow programme to improve water supply and sewerage that would take decades to complete.

Initially the board consisted of twelve members, four of whom faced re-election every year. In the election for 1859–60 for example, perhaps not surprisingly, the shopkeepers at the unpopular company stores, Joseph Rusher, Garnlwyd, and George Saunders, Llynfi Works, failed to gain a place on the Board of Health, with by far the lowest number of votes cast. After 1860 the managers and mineral agents at the local works became active board members. John Phanuel Roe, the Llynfi Works manager, was elected in 1860, and James Colquhoun in August 1869. James Barrow (1838–1902), the colliery agent for Brogden & Sons in the valley, also became actively involved in local government during the 1870s. Barrow, a native of Lancashire, came to Tondu with the Brogdens in about 1855 as a very young man and, at the time of the 1861 census, he was the mineral agent at the Tywith Colliery of Brogden & Sons. As outlined in an earlier chapter, James Barrow, who lived at Fairfield Cottage in the town centre, became a colliery proprietor in the 1880s and 1890s. He was also a well-known mining consultant around the turn of the century with a nationwide practice. James Barrow played an important role in the general life of the township and was the first chairman of the newly-formed Maesteg Urban District Council in 1894. He was listed as a Welsh speaker in the 1901 census, a measure of his commitment to his adopted home district.

Although the Board of Health established a basic form of 'town planning' in the district, introduced street lighting and attempted to improve the system of drainage and sewerage, progress was slow. Three decades later in 1893, the Sanitary Survey of Glamorganshire highlighted the urgent public health problems that needed to be addressed in the Maesteg area. Improvements in water storage and water supply were required and it was also suggested that the small local slaughter houses should be closed and replaced by a central abattoir. In addition, refuse disposal was regarded as inadequate and a more efficient system of drainage and sewerage was urgently required. In 1894 the new Maesteg Urban District Council began to address the concerns outlined in the Sanitary Survey of the previous year.

The formation of the Urban District Council coincided with other changes in the valley which combined to mark the beginning of a new era of growth and relative prosperity in the district. After the Llynvi, Tondu & Ogmore Coal & Iron Co. opted for voluntary liquidation in 1878, the efforts of John J. Smith, the receiver, had ensured there was a limited but significant industrial base in the valley during the lean years of the 1880s. He had been instrumental in forming the Llynvi & Tondu Co. in 1880, and that enterprise produced coal and iron until the demise of the company and the closure of the Llynfi Works in 1885. In the latter part of that decade he was also, rather controversially, responsible for bringing the coal reserves of the area to the attention of Colonel John North, the 'Nitrate King'. After an assessment of the mineral wealth of the district by the eminent mining engineer, T. Forster-Brown, the colonel and his associates formed North's Navigation Collieries (1889) Ltd. The initiatives of the new company transformed the Llynfi Valley in the period 1890–1910.

CHAPTER SIX

NORTH'S NAVIGATION COLLIERIES (1889) LTD

Maesteg had been built around the iron industry with an emphasis on the production of railway iron. After the collapse of iron making in the district, the Llynfi Valley, after a decade of uncertainty, found itself well-placed to benefit from another phase of the revolution in transportation, the steam coal boom. Although steam had powered vessels for much of the nineteenth century, up to the 1870s steam ships were fairly small, and sail was still of great importance. The development of steam shipping was hampered as the early marine engines were inefficient and consumed great quantities of coal. In the 1870s triple expansion marine steam engines were developed which were much more powerful and used coal more efficiently. As a consequence, steam ships were larger and faster, global trade increased spectacularly and communications improved between the larger European powers and their colonies. The development of the new generation of marine steam engines marked the end of the large-scale use of sail and created a vast demand for the types of coal that were well-suited to steam raising. There were substantial reserves of such coal in Glamorgan and Monmouthshire; the development of those reserves transformed the South Wales area in the years 1880–1910.

In 1882 John North returned to Britain after many years in South America. By the late 1880s he was a well-known figure around the London financial markets and was considering investing some of his considerable wealth in Turkish coal mines when J.J. Smith, coincidentally a neighbour of North in Eltham, Kent, brought the ailing Llynvi & Tondu Co. to his attention. He soon decided to make the company a major element in a series of worldwide investments that included gold mines in Australia, tramways in Egypt and cement manufacture in Belgium.

The story of North's Navigation Collieries (1889) Ltd and the rapid development of the Llynfi Valley in the years 1890–1910, has unlikely beginnings in the deserts of northern Chile and southern Peru. It was there that John Thomas North accumulated the fortune that enabled him to invest in the steam coal trade.

North was born in Holbeck near Leeds in 1842, the son of a prosperous coal merchant. In 1857 he was apprenticed as an engineer with Shaw, North & Watson of Hunslet and in 1865 he joined Fowler & Co., engineers, of Leeds. Two years later he was sent to Chile by the engineering firm to supervise locomotive construction for the Carrizal Co. in the copper mining zone near Caldera. He left Fowler & Co. in 1871 and worked in southern Peru at a time when nitrate production was increasing, and the industry was about to become important on a global scale.

The nitrates of the deserts of western South America became a great source of fertilizer after the depletion of Peruvian guano resources in the 1860s. By the mid-1870s annual nitrate exports had trebled in less than a decade, and both the Peruvian and Chilean governments viewed nitrate production as a major source of revenue. As the industry developed, North, in partnership with Maurice Jewell, the British vice-consul in the booming port of Iquique, imported nitrate-processing machinery and became involved in the supply of water to the desert township. By 1878 he had acquired a nitrate works, and had become a major partner in a company that supplied water to the nitrate region by ship. If the development of the desert lands had continued without interruption, John North would probably have ended his career as a reasonably prosperous entrepreneur in Peru. However, the development of the nitrate industry was transformed by the War of the Pacific (1879–83) between Chile and an alliance of Peru and Bolivia. The war also transformed the fortunes of John T. North and presented him with the opportunities to become a very wealthy man.

Some years before the war, in 1876, Peru had nationalised its nitrate enterprises and compensated the owners with bonds. The bonds would yield 8 per cent from the government for two years, then, when revenue became available, the owners would be paid in full. However, the Peruvian government could not raise the revenue to redeem the bonds, so when war broke out there were large numbers of the nitrate certificates in circulation in Peru. In the early days of the war, which was fought in the nitrate lands of southern Peru, North had already become the sole owner of the water supply company, his partners having fled the conflict. By 1881 the war had greatly reduced the value of the nitrate bonds and North, gambling on a victory for Chile, bought up large numbers of the certificates at low cost. The scheme was probably funded by loans authorised by John Dawson, the head of the Iquique branch of the Bank of Valparaiso, and North was advised by another associate, Robert Harvey, who had considerable knowledge of the Peruvian nitrate industry. Chile was eventually victorious and occupied the Peruvian nitrate district. North soon became the dominant figure in the nitrate trade when the Chilean government, anxious to quickly re-establish the lucrative nitrate industry, dramatically increased the value of the nitrate certificates by announcing that it would recognise the bonds as proof of ownership of the nitrate companies.

Some historians suggest that North had 'inside information' about the intentions of the Chilean government if they occupied the Peruvian nitrate lands. Others stress North's skill in organising and financing the scheme and emphasise his tendency to take calculated risks. Whatever the viewpoint there is no documentary evidence, no 'smoking gun', to suggest that North or his associate, Robert Harvey, had any knowledge of Chilean plans for the nitrate lands. The outcome of the episode was that John North became the key figure in the South American nitrate trade, with important connections with two-thirds of the nitrate companies, and the sobriquet 'The Nitrate King'.

On his return to Britain in 1882 with the highly valued bonds, he set up the Liverpool Nitrate Co. That company plus two others, the Colorado Nitrate Co., and the Primitiva Nitrate Co. formed the core of his nitrate production interests. He also had major shareholdings in a number of other nitrate companies including the Lagunas and the Paccha-Jazpampa ventures. By selling the properties he had acquired with the bonds, for up to ten times what he paid for them, and by taking enormous dividends in the 1880s nitrates boom from his own companies, the 'Nitrate King' accumulated a considerable fortune. In addition to his nitrate production companies, North had gained control of the Tarapaca Waterworks Co., the Nitrate Railway Co., and the Bank of Tarapaca & London. Thus, by the late 1880s, John T. North was the key figure in the economic development of a large area of northern Chile.

North acquired a mansion at Avery Hill in Eltham in 1883 and spared no expense in renovating and enlarging it. He held extravagant dinner parties, became a leading figure in London society and supported a range of sports. He was a successful breeder of greyhounds and racehorses, he sponsored boxing tournaments, and the great W.G. Grace dedicated his book, *The History of a Hundred Centuries*, to North. He also made large charitable contributions to the city of Leeds; he purchased Kirkstall Abbey for the city and funded hospital building. John North was given the Freedom of the Borough of Leeds in 1889. Nearer his home he equipped a regiment of volunteers in the Tower Hamlets district of east London, hence his honorary title of 'Colonel'. Today, North's mansion forms part of the Avery Hill Campus at the University of Greenwich.

During the 1880s, with his reputation for making money, his connections in South America and his down-to-earth approach to complex financial matters, the colonel became a successful manipulator of the nitrate market on the London Stock Exchange. The *Financial News* commented: 'put North's name on a costermonger's cart, turn it into a limited liability company, and the shares will be selling at 300 per cent premium before they are an hour old'.

During the nitrates boom of the mid-1880s North realised that the bubble was likely to burst, so he diversified into a range of enterprises on a global scale, hence his interest in the Llynfi Valley. Although John North had gained a reputation as a colourful, 'larger than life' character in the 1880s, he was, essentially, a quick-thinking, well-organised entrepreneur with a keen eye for a business opportunity. He demonstrated a range of skills when he acquired the extensive properties of the Llynvi & Tondu Co. for a knock-down price in June 1888. Although the story of the sale of the Llynfi company to North's colliery venture is a complex one, it can be outlined from a range of contemporary sources.

John Thomas North, founder of North's Navigation Collieries (1889) Ltd.

The ownership of the Llynvi & Tondu Co. was disputed in the High Court in 1885 when a complicated argument arose among the debenture holders. As a result of the legal action, the company became the subject of a court order. Court orders were then issued to wind up the venture in January 1887 and, in September that year, the property was put up for sale by tender. At that time Colonel John North became involved in the story and made a bid for the property of the Llynvi & Tondu Co. He arranged the transaction with his neighbour at Eltham, John Joseph Smith, the company receiver. In June 1888 North's low offer of £150,000 was accepted by the debenture holders and was sanctioned by a court order. The 'Nitrate King' then lived up to his reputation as a shrewd operator by transferring the Llynfi property to a new company he had quickly formed, the Western Navigation Collieries Syndicate Ltd. He then proceeded to assemble a major new company, North's Navigation Collieries (1889) Ltd, which was floated with a capital of £450,000, comprising 80,000 £5 Ordinary Shares, of which 56,000 were publicly subscribed, and 10,000 £5 Preferential Shares. Shortly afterwards, the colonel sold the former Llynvi & Tondu property to North's Navigation for £350,000 and wound up the Western syndicate. North had thus made a large profit on the transaction and was also the major shareholder, and the chairman, of North's Navigation Collieries Ltd. In addition, the large share issue had generated the capital required to develop the property.

John Joseph Smith's involvement in the negotiations was controversial, as he had been the receiver of the Llynvi & Tondu Co. when it was sold for £150,000, and later became an associate of the colonel in North's Navigation. After the resale of the property for such a large sum, Smith was challenged in the High Court in October 1889 by a small group of discontented former shareholders of the Llynvi & Tondu Co. Although the judge was concerned by J.J. Smith's dual role in the proceedings, he was cleared of any malpractice. Thus after a great deal of manoeuvring, a major new colliery enterprise emerged from the failure of the Llynvi & Tondu Co. Due largely to the initiatives of North's new company, the local coal industry expanded rapidly and the population of the Maesteg area increased from 9,000 in 1891 to 29,000 in 1921.

The properties which North's Navigation Collieries Ltd took over in 1889 consisted of the Wyndham and Tynewydd collieries in the Ogmore Valley, the Park Slip drift mine near Aberkenfig, the Tondu Ironworks, the Llynfi Ironworks in Maesteg and three collieries in the Llynfi Valley: Coegnant, No.9 Level and Maesteg Deep. Although the new company produced iron at Tondu until 1896, the demolition of the Llynfi Ironworks began in 1890 as North's concentrated on the development of its coal resources in the Maesteg district.

The South American connection was evident in the management of the new venture. Robert Harvey, a key associate of the colonel in Peru and Chile, became a director of North's, and his younger brother, John Boyd Harvey, who had returned from South America with his Peruvian wife, Julieta, became general manager in 1892. The Boyd Harveys lived for many years at Tondu House.

Soon after its formation, the company embarked on a programme of expansion. In 1891, 350 men were employed at the No.9 Level and 586 at Coegnant. Sinking was taking place at the large new colliery at Caerau and 137 were employed there. Only forty were listed for Maesteg Deep and records refer to 'drifting' taking place. It is possible that the original drift at the site was being driven down a gradient of 1:6 to reach the *Two Feet Nine* seam in 1890-1.

An account of day-to-day activity at North's collieries in 1890 exists at the Glamorgan Record Office. Every fortnight the firm of Forster-Brown & Rees, mining and civil engineers, filed reports to the company regarding progress at the collieries. The report for the fortnight to 1 March 1890 survives in the county archives. At the No.9 Level there were twelve working days during that two-week period, average output per day was 304 tons, and total output was 3,647 tons, a 15 per cent increase on the previous fortnight. There were only nine working days at Coegnant; average output per day was 516½ tons, and the total output was 4,649 tons, a 30 per cent reduction from the totals for the previous fortnight. Days were 'lost' due to a dispute over payment for small coal at the pit. Of the coal produced at No.9, 49 per cent was classed as 'large'; for Coegnant the proportion was 70 per cent. There was no production at Maesteg Deep, and it was noted in the report that: 'drifting is making satisfactory progress and the arching through the fall is progressing as well as can be expected in the circumstances'. Sinking was in progress at Caerau where it was reported that: 'the North Pit is down nineteen yards on to a bed of fireclay, should this turn out well the first length of walling may be commenced this week…' It was also noted that 'the railway from Coegnant is proceeding steadily'.

During the early 1890s the company made steady progress in the coal trade. By 1893, for example, North's had established a firm foothold in the London house coal market despite the efforts of the London 'coal ring' to block the company's entry into the metropolitan coal trade. Colonel North was determined to challenge the 'ring', and his company, initially, succeeded in supplying house coal to Messrs Radford's depots in Paddington, Camden and Chelsea. By January 1894 North's challenge to the members of the 'coal ring' had become a major issue in the metropolitan coal trade. In the face of a boycott from a number of coal merchants, North set up his own house coal depots at Paddington, Chelsea and Brentford, and coal was delivered directly to the customer. The *Pall Mall Gazette* reported that,

> …the ring has reduced the price of best coal, but North's Navigation supplies are 6s a ton cheaper. It now remains to be seen whether, given a good article at a fair price, the ring has the power to successfully boycott a colliery owner who declines to be coerced. Colonel North is not a man who surrenders easily, and his opponents will yet discover he has power enough to win the fight…

Although North's Navigation had quickly established itself as major producer of high-quality coal, the first years of the enterprise were difficult ones. In 1892 one of the worst mining disasters in South Wales occurred at the company's Park Slip Colliery when 112 men were killed in an explosion. From April 1894 to February 1896 there was a dispute over wage rates at the new Caerau Colliery, which checked the early progress of the company. In May 1896 Colonel North died of a heart attack while chairing a meeting of the Buena Ventura Co. in London; he was fifty-four. In the months before his death he had continued to add to his global interests by promoting the development of Ostend as a fashionable holiday resort in association with King Leopold II of the Belgians. Although John North had only been associated with the district for a short time, his investment had re-vitalised the Maesteg area after the uncertainty of the 1880s. He was commemorated by the building of the Colonel North Memorial Hall in the town centre which was completed in 1899.

Due largely to the prolonged strike at Caerau Colliery, profits began to slump in 1894, but after the settlement of the dispute in February 1896, the progress of the company was spectacular. Between 1895 and 1897 coal output increased 51 per cent and passed 1 million tons for the first time in the latter year.

In 1897 the opening of the Port Talbot Railway and the Vale of Glamorgan Railway (VoGR) to Barry gave the company access to those ports at relatively low cost, and, with growing demand for the company's coal, dividends to shareholders were increasing. Both railway ventures had been actively promoted by Colonel North and his colliery company in the early 1890s. The colonel became directly involved in the development of the VoGR after the Great Western Railway had refused to grant favourable freight rates to North's Navigation in the late 1880s.

By 1899, 2,286 men were employed by the company in the Llynfi Valley, almost double the figure for 1891. Caerau Colliery, the largest in the district with 862 workers, had been sunk to the *Six Feet* steam coal seam and was well-established, and Coegnant, Maesteg Deep and the No.9 Level were in full production.

As a measure of the success of the company, the share capital was increased from £450,000 to £650,000 in 1903. The new share issue was sanctioned by a local Act of Parliament in June of that year. Because of the profits that had accrued, especially during the years 1899–1901, and the returns on the investment of the company's reserve fund in government securities, North's re-valued its assets and distributed 40,000 new, paid-up, £5 ordinary shares to existing holders. Some years later, in April 1914, the company's ordinary shares were divided into £1 units, and were further divided into 5s units in November 1916.

During 1903–4 Coegnant Colliery was modernised, and deepened to the *Bute (Lower New)* seam. The redevelopment included the widening of the shafts, for example the diameter of the South Pit was increased from 9½ft to 20ft. In 1904 North's Navigation received a major boost when coal from Caerau Colliery was included on the prestigious 'Admiralty List' of the best steam coals. The company sold its collieries outside the Maesteg area in 1906 and concentrated production at the four sites in the Llynfi Valley, with coal washeries and coke ovens at Maesteg Deep and Tondu. The collieries were connected by North's own railway system and, in later years, the company's electricity grid would link the mines. In February 1908 a third shaft was completed at the Caerau site; known as the No.3 Pit, it was sunk to the general-purpose *Caedefaid* seam at 167 yards. In just eight years from 1899 to 1907 the workforce at North's pits in the Llynfi Valley had almost doubled to 4,300 and the expansion was far from complete.

The impact of the coal boom on the valley's communities was spectacular. The scale of change in the upper Llynfi Valley over a relatively short period can be seen in the graph on page 44. Caerau (or Spelter), which up to the late 1880s had consisted of Tonna Road, Metcalfe Street, Toncwd Row and scattered housing, was transformed into a large mining community.

A survey of mining settlement in South Wales, published in 1969, describes how the new community of Caerau was built up. Unlike the iron companies which built rows of houses for the workforce in Maesteg and Nantyffyllon during the 1840s, North's had little direct involvement in the housing of its colliers. The company built just one row – North Street in Caerau. About half of the remaining houses were built by speculators and half were built by building clubs set up by the workforce. Nantyffyllon, which was already an established industrial community by 1860, was less spectacularly affected by North's developments.

There are also references to the build-up of housing in Caerau in a North's Navigation record book that survives at the National Library of Wales. In the book, which was presumably compiled by the company's estates' department, it was noted that, in the late 1890s, the Caerau Building Society Ltd was constructing sixty houses in the Victoria Road area, and land for 163 houses had been leased from J.P. Treharne on the north side of Caerau Road. Reference was also made to the building of seventy-three new houses in Hermon Road.

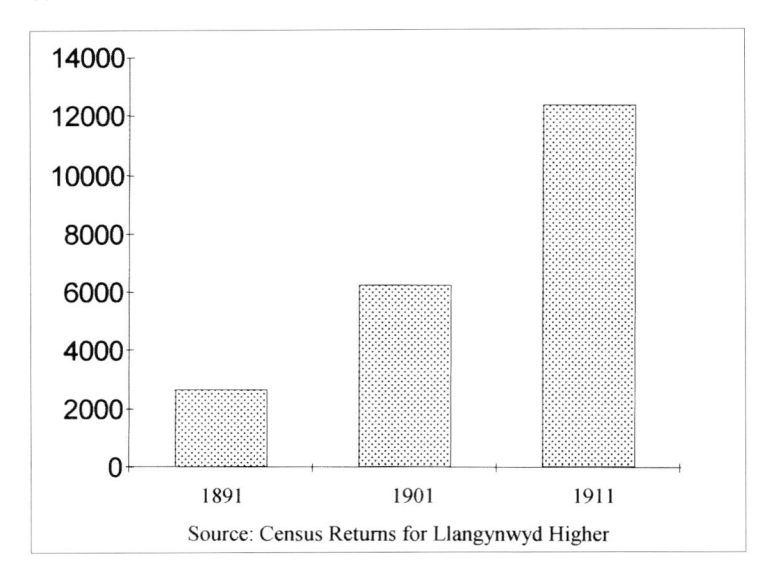

Graph showing population change in Nantyffyllon and Caerau 1891–1911.

From reports in the *Glamorgan Gazette* during the early years of the twentieth century, the first bank was opened in the growing township in April 1902 when a branch of the Metropolitan Bank at Maesteg opened for business in Caerau. In 1903 the newspaper reported that, because of the growing population, a new Caerau Ward would be created at the head of the valley with four representatives on the Maesteg Urban District Council. As a result of the creation of the new ward, council membership increased from twelve to sixteen. Two years later, on Saturday 17 June 1905, the Caerau Miners' Institute was officially opened by Mrs Jones the wife of the local colliery manager, County Councillor Jenkin Jones. It was reported that the building had cost £2,495, of which £1,300 had been contributed by the colliers via a levy of 1½d per week and £300 had been given by North's Navigation, leaving a debt of about £900 on the building. It was noted in the *Gazette* that 'the workmen hope to wipe this sum out at an early date'.

Two miles to the south of the Caerau pits, North's Navigation continued to expand with the development of a large new colliery on the site of the old Cwmdu levels originally worked by R.P. Lemon & Co. On 31 July 1908 the *Glamorgan Gazette* reported that John Boyd Harvey's daughter, Doña Duarte y Moreno of Malaga, Spain, had 'cut the first sod' of the downcast pit in a formal ceremony to mark the commencement of sinking. During the ceremony Doña Duarte named the new venture 'St John's Colliery', and gave reasons for the choice of the name. She mentioned that 'St John's' was appropriate as John was the christian name of both Colonel North, the founder of the company, and J.J. Smith the company chairman. She added that it was also the name of her father's Patron Saint. By 1911, two shafts had been sunk to the *Bute (Lower New)* seam at 383 yards. As the new site was developed, North's oldest mine, the No.9 Level (or Caedefaid Colliery), was closed. The company planned to gain access to coal reserves below the No.9 workings from St. John's.

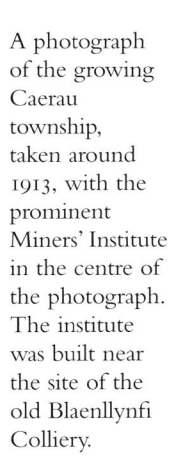

A photograph of the growing Caerau township, taken around 1913, with the prominent Miners' Institute in the centre of the photograph. The institute was built near the site of the old Blaenllynfi Colliery.

At the time when coal exports from South Wales reached peak levels, in 1913, North's Navigation Collieries (1889) Ltd was ranked among the ten largest colliery companies in the county with about 5,500 workers. In 1916 the Caerau Colliery site was the fifth largest in Glamorgan. Only the Cambrian Pits and the Glamorgan Coal Co.'s pits at Llwynypia, Rhondda, the Merthyr Vale Pits at Aberfan and the Llanbradach Pits employed more. Due to geological difficulties the development of St John's Colliery was delayed until 1918 at considerable cost to the company. However, the two steam coal collieries at Caerau and Coegnant were very successful in the years leading up to the First World War due to the natural qualities of the coal and the efficient way it was prepared for the customer. From the early years of the company, when the first mechanical screening plant in South Wales was installed at Caerau Colliery, there had been considerable investment in screening and grading plants at the collieries and at the company's Tondu washery.

The names of North's customers during the years 1912–16 are listed in a company stock book at the Glamorgan Record Office. In 1912 J.J. Smith, who had taken over the chairmanship after Colonel North's death in 1896, was still chairman of the company. The board of directors included Sir Robert Harvey (who had been knighted in 1901), John Boyd Harvey and G.H. Lockett, the Liverpool nitrate importer. The South American connection was still significant in 1912 as North's supplied coal to the Nitrate Railways Co. in Chile, the Colorado Nitrate Co. and the Liverpool Nitrate Co.

The link with the Chilean nitrate industry was a distinctive feature of the early development of North's Navigation Collieries. Messrs Smith, Lockett and Harvey were directors of three of the largest nitrate companies and a trading pattern between North's and the nitrate producers was established in the mid-1890s. Trade increased with the development of Port Talbot Docks and, by 1904,

Iquique, the main port of the nitrate lands, was the chief destination for coal ships sailing from Port Talbot. North's supplied the Chilean nitrate works, and the locomotives on the 380-mile network of the Nitrate Railways Co. in northern Chile were fuelled by Llynfi Valley coal. Ironically for a steam coal producer, most of the coal exported by North's to Chile was carried by large four-masted sailing ships on voyages around Cape Horn that often took three months. The largest of the vessels were known as the 'Nitrate Clippers' and were owned by the famous French firm of A.D. Bordes. The sailing ships left Port Talbot with local coal for Iquique, returning with nitrate cargoes for the European ports. The trade with the nitrate lands seems to have peaked at the end of the Edwardian period and, by the beginning of the First World War, the Chilean market was much less important for North's Navigation. At that time exports to Iquique, for example, had declined by 50 per cent due to wartime restrictions on the coal trade and the introduction of fuel oil in the nitrate lands.

From listings in the stock book, by 1915 major buyers of the company's coal were the Italian Navy, HM Government, the Russian Navy, the Union Castle Mail Steamship Co. and the Tug Coaling Syndicate. Before the First World War, Deutsches Kohlen-Depot, an association of the leading German shipping companies such as the Hamburg–Amerika Line and Norddeutscher–Lloyd had been a major customer; a considerable sum, for coal purchased before the conflict, had to be written off by North's early in 1915. By 1916 coal output was dominated by the war effort; by far the largest customer was HM Government in that year. Steam coal for the Admiralty and foundry coke for government factories and munitions works were in great demand. Apart from British government agencies, other important buyers in 1916 were the Italian Navy, Italian State Railways and the French Navy.

Before the First World War, North's coal was mainly exported from Port Talbot and Barry. From sales records for 1912 for example, 74 per cent of the company's large coal stocks at the ports was at Port Talbot with 23 per cent at Barry and relatively small amounts at Cardiff, Swansea, Newport and Portsmouth. Coal export figures for Port Talbot for 1912 give some indication of the main export markets served by the Llynfi Valley collieries during the heyday of the South Wales coal trade. Just over a third (36 per cent) of coal exports were for western France, 18 per cent for the Mediterranean, 15 per cent of coal shipments were for the coast of north-west Europe from Hamburg to Brest, and 12 per cent was exported to Chile. The main ports receiving coal from Port Talbot in 1912 were Bordeaux (14 per cent of coal exported), Zeebrugge, Belgium (10 per cent), Genoa, Italy (9 per cent), Valparaiso, Chile (6 per cent), St Nazaire, France (5 per cent) and Iquique, Chile (3 per cent). Frequent callers at Port Talbot and other South Wales ports before the First World War were ships of 'The Nitrate Producers' Steamship Co. Ltd', a shipping line that was partly financed by Colonel North in 1893. The steamers were known as 'The Nitrate Boats' and carried John North's racing colours in the form of blue and red bands (with a yellow star) on the funnels.

As an efficient enterprise with large modern collieries and a reputation for producing Admiralty-grade steam coal, excellent foundry coke and first-class house coal, North's inevitably attracted the attention of the colliery combines that had grown by absorbing smaller producers. The Cambrian Combine, built up by Lord Rhondda, took over North's in October 1916, although the company name was retained. The combine paid £1,200,000 for the Llynfi Valley Co., purchasing all of North's 600,000 ordinary £1 shares at £2 each. The take-over of 1916 marked the end of J. J. Smith's long association with the industrial development of the Llynfi Valley although a family connection was maintained as his son, J. Wentworth Smith, joined the board of North's Navigation on his father's retirement. John Joseph Smith was the chairman of North's from 1896 until he retired, aged seventy-nine, at the time of the take-over; he died in June 1921. The new board of directors included some of the leading figures in the South Wales coal trade including Lord Rhondda's daughter, Viscountess Rhondda, H. Seymour Berry, Sir Archibald Mitchelson, and D.R. Llewellyn who became chairman of North's Navigation in 1924.

The peak employment totals for North's collieries were reached during the period 1921–4. In the former year 6,359 worked in the company's collieries and in 1924 the figure was 6,052. St John's was finally in full production and the two Caerau steam coal shafts had been deepened to the *Bute (Lower New)* seam. Annual production from the four colliery sites was about 1,300,000 tons. The year 1924 effectively marked the end of three decades of spectacular growth by both the company and the Maesteg Urban District. The 1921 census placed the district, with a population of almost 29,000, among the larger urban districts in Wales.

North's Navigation seems to have retained its independence when many famous colliery companies in South Wales were absorbed by the giant combinations that were created in the 1920s and 1930s. In 1929 a large number of colliery companies amalgamated to form Welsh Associated Collieries Ltd, and Welsh Associated then merged with the Powell Duffryn grouping in 1935. For reasons which are not clear, all the companies under the chairmanship of D.R. Llewellyn, except North's Navigation, became part of Welsh Associated Collieries in 1929. Sixteen years later, in 1945, North's ceased trading as an independent venture when it became part of the Powell Duffryn Group. From contemporary press reports, although some of North's Navigation shares had been held for a number of years by Powell Duffryn, the colliery combine purchased the remaining shares, and thus acquired the 'effective ownership' of North's, in May 1945. Just nineteen months later, in January 1947, the coal industry was nationalised.

CHAPTER SEVEN

ELDER'S NAVIGATION COLLIERIES LTD

Although it could be argued that Maesteg had become a 'company town' during the Edwardian period due to the initiatives of North's Navigation Collieries, the Garth and Oakwood pits were also significant employers. During the 1890s Garth employed about 500 workers and Oakwood around 400. They were both worked with limited success by James Barrow & Associates until the collieries were put up for sale in March 1898. Just as the steam coal boom and the mineral wealth of the valley had brought Colonel North's investment capital to the district in 1889, another remarkable entrepreneur, the shipping magnate, Alfred Jones, began to take an interest in Llynfi Valley steam coal ten years later. In 1899 Jones, who had gained control of the large fleets operated by Elder Dempster Shipping Ltd, made an unsuccessful attempt to buy Garth and Oakwood before eventually completing the transaction early in 1900.

From press reports, the transfer of the Garth and Oakwood properties was a complex one, with the collieries changing hands twice before Alfred Jones, who was knighted in 1900, finally acquired the mines for £85,000. After the initial deal with Alfred Jones fell through in May 1899, the collieries were bought by the Victoria Investment Corporation. The investment corporation had bought the mines to quickly sell again, and it was in renewed negotiations with Elder Dempster early in January 1900. Once again the deal fell through and another major shipping venture, Furness Withy & Co., began to show an interest in the collieries. Furness Withy bought Garth and Oakwood, probably at the end of January, and the saga ended shortly afterwards when, for reasons which are not clear, Furness Withy then sold the mines to Elder Dempster and Sir Alfred Jones.

Alfred Lewis Jones was born in Carmarthen in 1845 and grew up in Liverpool, his family having moved there when he was three years old. As a young man he was employed in the shipping industry, and over a number of years he established himself as a leading figure in the commercial life of the Mersey port. By the mid-1880s he had gained a controlling interest in the Elder Dempster Shipping Co. at a time when the new generation of steam ships was transforming world trade and improving communication links between Britain and the colonies.

An advertisement for the 'parent company' of Elder's Navigation Collieries Ltd, c. 1910.

Sir Alfred Jones' shipping company specialised in the tropical African trade and he established Elder Dempster as a major influence on the commercial development of 'British West Africa' during the 1880s. At that time the West African territories were little more than outposts, with little infrastructure and few services. As a result of the initiatives of Sir Alfred, his company's agents along the West African coast provided a range of basic services including banking. As trade developed in the 1880s and 1890s, Alfred Jones' fleet of steamers increased spectacularly. In 1884, for example, Elder Dempster owned thirty-five vessels (total tonnage 53,000); by 1900 there were eighty-seven ships in the fleet (total tonnage 269,000). During the 1880s there was thus a need for coaling stations to fuel the growing number of steamers on the West African routes. The Canary Islands were strategically placed between Britain and West Africa and Elder Dempster set up important coaling stations there. As trade increased during the 1890s, the enterprising Sir Alfred, not wishing to depend on agencies outside his immediate control, decided to acquire his own supplies of steam coal, hence his interest in the Llynfi Valley. By producing his own fuel Jones could supply his own shipping and, at the same time, he could regulate the coal trade along the West African coast.

Sir Alfred Jones, shrewdly noting the run-down condition of farming in the sub-tropical Canaries and the faster journey times of the new generation of steam ships, encouraged banana production in the islands and introduced and marketed the fruit in Britain for the first time in the 1890s. For that reason the resourceful Sir Alfred was known as 'The Banana King' at the time of the purchase of his Llynfi Valley collieries.

Sir Alfred Jones' colliery venture traded as Elder's Navigation Collieries Ltd and the new company was incorporated on 7 March 1900 with a nominal capital of £50,000 in 5,000 shares of £10. Sir Alfred Jones held almost all the shares and there were, initially, only two directors: Sir Alfred and his associate William John Davey, a Liverpool steam ship owner.

Some of the shipping company's reasons for selecting the Garth and Oakwood collieries were outlined in 'Ocean Highways', a publication issued by Elder Dempster & Co. in 1901. The reputation of 'the Garth coal', especially the house coal of the *Two Feet Nine* seam, was an important factor as the company expected the lower, largely untapped, steam coal seams to be of the same high quality. Perhaps of equal importance was the nearness of the collieries to the newly developed docks at Port Talbot. The publication claimed that coal from Elder's two collieries 'could be put aboard ships at Port Talbot within two hours of its despatch from the pit mouth'.

The mines at Garth and Oakwood were in need of modernisation in 1900 and the new company soon deepened the workings to the *Bute (Lower New)* seam and completely redeveloped the surface at Garth. No expense seems to have been spared on the modernisation of the Garth Pits as Sir Alfred Jones created a showpiece colliery on the site. A large new washery plant was installed there as well as banks of modern Coppee coke ovens. The head frame towers of both the Garth Pits were replaced, and the coal was conveyed from the pit-head to the screens by a new self-acting tramway. Many of the ramshackle surface buildings were replaced by well-designed winding-engine houses, stores and workshops, all 'built of Fforchlas Pennant stone and faced with Cattybrook bricks'. The new range of buildings had a total frontage of 100 yards. The eminent mining engineer, Professor William Galloway of the University of Wales in Cardiff, was the consultant who reorganised the Garth operation.

About 300,000 tons of coal and 50,000 tons of coke were produced annually during the years 1904–8, and in 1907 just over 1,000 workers were employed at Garth with 123 at Oakwood. As coke production was centralised at Garth, the forty-nine beehive coke ovens that extended for 150 yards to the south of the Oakwood Colliery gradually became redundant and were dismantled. In 1906 a feature on Elder's two collieries in the *Syren and Shipping Illustrated* included a comment that the two mines, which were just 900m apart, were operated as one unit with the Waddle Fan at the Oakwood No.2 (upcast) Pit ventilating the workings of both collieries. This was probably a temporary arrangement during the redevelopment of the property as, some years later in 1917, a 24ft Waddle Fan was listed at Garth.

Elder's collieries supplied coaling stations in the Canary Islands, steam coal was exported to West Africa and coke, house coal and steam coal were produced for the British market. The link between the Garth and Oakwood collieries and the Canary Islands in the Edwardian era was a strong one. Elder's Navigation Collieries exported large quantities of coal to Las Palmas, Gran Canaria, and to Santa Cruz, Tenerife, where it was stock-piled for use by the steamers of the Elder Dempster Line. The firm's coal was also marketed and sold through the Grand Canary Coaling Co., Jones' sales agency in Las Palmas. During the period 1900 to 1910 the two Llynfi Valley collieries undoubtedly made an important contribution to the rapidly increasing coal trade of the Canary Islands and to the consequent expansion of Puerto de la Luz, the port of Las Palmas.

A 'classic' view of a South Wales mining community at Garth from around 1912, with Libanus Chapel (1871), (left), and the Miners' Institute of 1910, (centre), together with terraced housing.

Coaling an Elder Dempster vessel at Port Talbot Docks around 1901. Bunker coal was loaded by dockside crane (left), from bags (centre) and by wheel-barrow (right). The ship was described as a 'transport' and was probably a Boer War troop ship.

Although Elder's coal was not on the 'Admiralty List', it was in great demand as a well-known 'Best Cardiff' steam coal. It is therefore probable that the company's output was supplied to shipping companies other than Elder Dempster. This seems likely as, in the Edwardian era, the Grand Canary Coaling Co. supplied bunker coal to 200 steamship lines as well as the German, French, Brazilian and Italian Navies. Also, in 1909, as we can see from advertisements in the trade press, Elder's Navigation had agencies in a number of European ports. The company's agent at Le Havre, for example, was the Cunard Steamship Co., and Elder's Southampton agents, Nisbet & Co., were also agents for the Federal Line, the Atlantic Line and Compeigne Belge Maritime Du Congo. Unlike North's, which exported almost all its coal through the South Wales ports, Elder's also had coal stocks near the transatlantic liner terminals at Liverpool and Southampton.

Sir Alfred died in 1909 at a time when his collieries were in financial difficulties. Although a great deal of money had been spent by Elder's Navigation at the Garth and Oakwood sites, the mines had operated at a loss from 1900 to 1910; the losses were sustained by Sir Alfred Jones until the time of his death. Although it is difficult to account for the losses due to lack of contemporary information, it is possible that Sir Alfred's coal producing venture incurred 'acceptable' losses so that Elder Dempster, the parent company, could dominate both the coal trade in West Africa, and the supply of bunker coal to coaling stations along the West African routes. Alfred Jones effectively controlled the West African shipping trade from 1895 to 1909, and the provision of a reliable supply of coal from his own collieries could have been one of the many tactics he employed to sustain his trading monopoly. For example, Jones won contracts to supply coal to Nigeria by undercutting the existing price by 27 per cent per ton, and by undercutting the price tendered by his main competitor, Miller Bros, by 7 per cent. Such low prices allowed Sir Alfred Jones to dominate the coal trade in West Africa and any losses could have been sustained by the profitability of other Elder Dempster enterprises. After Sir Alfred's death the losses at the collieries became an issue and the mines were closed temporarily in 1910. Following a review of the situation by Elder Dempster, and after negotiations with the workforce over new pay rates, the pits were re-opened in November 1910.

In the same year, 1910, with the future of the two collieries in doubt, another shipping magnate, Sir Owen Philipps (Lord Kylsant), took control of the Elder Dempster shipping line. In December 1910 the mining subsidiary of the shipping company was restructured as Elder's Collieries Ltd with a new board of directors under the chairmanship of Lord Kylsant. The first priority for the re-formed company was to ensure the future of the two collieries by 'writing off' the considerable losses that had built up during the first ten years in production. The reorganisation of the company soon produced results and output reached 246,000 tons in 1913, an increase of 47 per cent over the figure for 1911. A few years later, in March 1915, at the Fifteenth Annual General Meeting of the company, it was reported that the fortunes of the enterprise had improved and modest profits had been made. At the same meeting it was decided to change the company name to

Celtic Collieries Ltd. In his address to shareholders the chairman gave the reason for the change:

> There are a good many Elders companies on the market and although we do not in any way object to being mistaken for any of them, at the same time we directors think it well to make this distinction, and that is why we suggested the change.

At the time of the next Annual General Meeting in March 1916, the company was paying record dividends of 10 per cent, and, after five successful years, Kylsant announced that he had accepted a very good offer for Celtic Collieries Ltd from Lord Rhondda's Cambrian Combine. The combine purchased the company's shares for £230,000 and the new company name was retained. H. Seymour Berry, a director of North's, took the place of Lord Kylsant as the chairman of Celtic Collieries Ltd and a number of the new directors were also board members of North's Navigation. By 1920 Celtic Collieries had again been restructured as a new joint stock company with a capital of £400,000 in 400,000 ordinary shares and 400,000 preferential shares at 10s each. There were almost 3,000 investors, a complete contrast to the years from 1900 to 1916 when firstly Sir Alfred Jones, then Lord Kylsant were by far the largest shareholders.

The years between 1916 and 1924 were the most successful in the history of the Garth and Oakwood collieries. During the First World War 'Celtic' coal was supplied to the Royal Navy, and, in 1922, the 'Celtic' brand was finally included on the Admiralty List of the thirty-three best steam coals. For a number of years the company paid dividends of 10 per cent, and about 650 were employed at Garth with 250 at Oakwood. During those years the company produced 200,000 tons of coal and 30,000 tons of coke per annum.

In 1920 North's Navigation made a substantial offer for Celtic Collieries Ltd. The matter was discussed at the Annual General Meeting on 9 March 1920, and the Celtic chairman, H. Seymour Berry, recommended North's offer to the shareholders. The Celtic mineral estate was held under lease from North's Navigation Collieries, and the leases were due to expire in December 1923. The chairman explained the situation to the shareholders:

> I would like to tell you that we hold our lease as a sub-lease from Messrs. North's Navigation, and this lease expires in December 1923. At that period, until March, 1924, the property would be in the possession of Messrs. North's Navigation Collieries. You will understand that we obtained a lease from March, 1924, for a further period, but you will also realise that there is an interval, and having regard to possibilities of expensive litigation and difficulties in settling, it was very advisable that we should come to terms with North's Navigation well in advance. That was the principal reason why we thought that in your interest it was advisable to link up with North's.

The chairman also informed the meeting that North's had offered the shareholders a substantial sum in cash and a share in North's Navigation Collieries. Not surprisingly the shareholders agreed to the merger.

CHAPTER EIGHT

THE HAZARDS OF MINING

Fortunately the Llynfi Valley avoided the mining catastrophes that were experienced by so many coalfield communities in South Wales. Two such disasters occurred in neighbouring areas: eighty-seven lives were lost at Morfa Colliery near Port Talbot in 1890, and two years later, 112 men died at Park Slip Colliery near Aberkenfig. The most serious mining accident in the Maesteg area occurred at the Gin Pit in 1863 when fourteen lives were lost. Eleven men died in an explosion at Oakwood Colliery in 1872 and nine miners were killed in a cage-winding accident at Garth Colliery in 1897.

Significantly, the two most serious accidents in the Maesteg area occurred during the earlier phase of mining, before the widespread use of safety lamps and before the introduction of fan-ventilation. The Gin Pit explosion was fully reported in *The Cambrian* and the *Bridgend Chronicle* in January 1864; the reports give a considerable amount of detail about working conditions at the time. The Gin Pit, a relatively small coal and iron-ore mine owned by the Llynvi Vale Iron Co., employed 163 men at the time of the accident early on Boxing Day 1863. The explosion was the result of a combination of factors. The pit was idle on Christmas Day so no checks had been made for a thirty-hour period before work was due to begin on Boxing Day. As a further complication, the overman responsible for inspecting the workings before the start of the shift was ill, and his deputy did not take on his duties as he was not informed of the overman's absence. At about 6.30 a.m. the men, in contravention of the colliery rules, entered the unchecked workings and walked to their workplaces. In the main part of the colliery the miners worked with locked Davy Lamps, but there were districts where safety lamps were not used. One such place was No. 10 stall which was at the furthest point in the workings. As the colliers entered that stall a naked light ignited the gas that had accumulated there and eleven men and three boys were killed as a consequence. All the victims were found in and around No. 10 stall. The mines' inspector commented on the considerable amount of burnt coal in the stall and on the severe force of the blast, which had 'doubled up' some iron trams near the coal face.

During the inquest the mines inspector, Mr Thomas Evans, recalled a previous visit to the Gin Pit when he found that the ventilation was poor and the colliery was in a 'most deplorable condition'. Since that visit the general manager of the Llynfi Ironworks, John Phanuel Roe, had improved the circulation of air in the pit and, at the time of the accident, the inspector stated that the furnace ventilation system was adequate. Mr Evans was concerned, however, that naked lights were used in the workings, and that the canvas brattices used to channel the air-flow around the pit had not been effectively installed near the scene of the explosion. He was also concerned about the rather casual system of management at the mine as the men, in contravention of colliery rules, were allowed to enter unchecked workings, and an overman could 'absent himself without informing his superiors'. In his summing-up the inspector stated: 'I do not think it safe to work in a colliery, in one part of which locked safety lamps are used, and in another part naked lights. I think that if on this occasion the men had had safety lamps probably the explosion would not have occurred'. He also emphasised 'the paramount importance of active supervision on the part of the manager of a colliery, and the intelligent cooperation on the part of his subordinates'. Despite the fact that the management at the Gin Pit had been criticised at the inquest, it was reported in the *Bridgend Chronicle* that: 'although there was culpable inattention, it was not so darkly coloured as to be pronounced criminal negligence'. Thus no blame was apportioned and a verdict of accidental death was returned.

At a time long before there was any system of assistance or compensation for the dependents of mine-accident victims, there is limited evidence that the Llynvi Vale Iron Co. offered some support to bereaved families after the Gin Pit explosion. It was reported in *The Times* of 7 January 1864, two weeks after the blast, that Stephen Wright Metcalfe, the chairman of the company, and John Phanuel Roe, the works' manager, had visited all the families affected by the disaster. Each family was given an assurance that the company would provide the same weekly income as the household had received before the explosion, 'until some settled arrangement should be made as to providing for them for the future'.

The causes of the other major colliery explosion in the district, the Oakwood blast of 10 January 1872, were not as clear-cut as the Gin Pit tragedy. The explosion occurred around midnight at a time, fortunately, when very few of the 140 miners employed at the colliery were at work. There were only eleven men working underground. Unlike the fairly localised Gin Pit blast eight years before, the more powerful Oakwood explosion ripped through the mine. All eleven miners, who were quite widely distributed through the workings along the *Upper Four Feet* seam, were killed. Such was the extent of the explosion that the flue-man at the ventilation furnace near the pit bottom, far from the source of the blast, was killed instantly. The sound of the explosion was heard across the valley as large amounts of debris erupted from the No.2 Pit shaft which was adjacent to the roadside in Bethania Street. Such was the force of the blast that the shaft cage was badly mangled, iron sheeting was strewn around the pit-head and the lamp-room roof was badly damaged. At the start of the shift thirteen men were underground; two men escaped with their lives when, having finished their work, they returned to the surface an hour or so before the blast.

With loss of life on such a scale, and as most of the victims had lived in a fairly small area of housing near the pit-head, the explosion had a devastating effect on many families and stunned a neighbourhood. Two young brothers were killed; one woman lost her husband and a brother in the accident; one of the victims was due to be married on the Saturday following the explosion. After the initial period of anguish and bewilderment, the community rallied in support of the bereaved. Neighbours supported young widows with children, and large crowds paid their respects at the funerals. Three of the victims were interred at Bethania burial ground and six at Llangynwyd. There were large numbers at Bethania and hundreds walked in procession to Llangynwyd where 'the roads leading to the church were everywhere full, although the rain poured incessantly'. Two of the victims were buried in Aberdare and Llantrisant, their home districts.

At the inquest on the eleven men, which was reported in the *Central Glamorgan Gazette,* witnesses described the events immediately after the blast, and also presented evidence about conditions underground in the days and hours leading up to the tragedy. One of the first to descend the pit after the explosion was James Barrow, the manager of the nearby Garth Colliery. After a few hours, despite the presence of lethal after-damp in the workings, Barrow, with a small team of assistants, courageously restored the ventilation system and attempted to recover the bodies. At 4.00 a.m. the first three of the victims were removed from the pit.

From the evidence of a number of witnesses including Mr T.H. Wales, the mines inspector, it seems that in the heading where the blast probably occurred, a 'blower' of gas had been detected in the days before the explosion. Although the gas had been dispersed, danger marks had been set in place and mine officials had been informed of the presence of gas. As a consequence, shot-firing had been suspended in that part of the workings. Although the furnace-ventilation of the pit was regarded as 'adequate' and locked safety lamps were used, the mines inspector was of the opinion that, just before the explosion, another 'sudden outburst of gas' had issued from a fissure near the heading. He was not clear, however, about the cause of ignition of quite a large volume of methane gas. There was speculation at the inquest and in the valley that one of the victims had, in contravention of colliery rules, fired an explosive charge in the heading, igniting the gas. Although there was some indication along the coal face that a shot had been fired, the mines inspector found it 'difficult to conceive how any man, even if not forbidden to do so, could have been so reckless as to fire a shot under such circumstances'. As the evidence was limited the jury concluded: 'We are of the opinion that the deceased were killed by an explosion of gas, but the evidence adduced is not sufficient to enable us to say how or by whom the gas was ignited'.

Although during the 1870s the mining workforce in the Llynfi Valley was relatively small compared to later years, the three-and-a-half-year period from January 1872 to August 1875 was marked by the highest incidence of serious accidents in the history of the Maesteg district. In addition to the eleven deaths at Oakwood, one man was killed and three were seriously burned at the old Cwmdu Colliery in April 1874, and three men died as a result of a fall at the Caedefaid Colliery (No.9 Level) at the end of August 1875.

The Cwmdu accident occurred because naked lights were still being used by colliers cutting coal in the mine as there was 'no history of gas in the workings'. The fatality and the serious injuries resulted when a 'blower' of gas, released by a small roof fall, was ignited by the candle-flame of a miner working nearby. The Caedefaid tragedy was another example of the almost 'casual' approach to many aspects of mine safety prevalent in the earlier period of mining. The three victims were members of a family that had recently arrived in the valley from Cornwall and, for some reason, all three were cutting coal in an isolated part of the workings. During the afternoon of Tuesday 31 August, while at the coal face, they were seriously injured by a fall, yet no one at the colliery knew of their plight, and they were not reported missing by their family when they failed to return home that evening. At about 7.00 a.m. the next day the fall was discovered by the duty fireman making a routine inspection of the workings, and the alarm was raised. One of the victims had died shortly after the fall of rock, about fifteen hours before the arrival of the fireman; a second died as he was carried out of the mine and the third died of his injuries at home that afternoon.

Conditions underground began to slowly improve in the late 1870s and the 1880s with the adoption of fan-ventilation at the collieries and the widespread use of locked safety lamps. Along with the advances in mining technology, important legislation such as the Coal Mines' Regulation Act of 1887 attempted to address the problem of safety underground. However, despite some improvement, the safety legislation was still inadequate. A major limitation of the 1887 Act, for example, was tragically exposed by the third major mining accident in the Llynfi Valley: the Garth Colliery overwind of 1897 which claimed nine lives.

The tragedy occurred around 5.00 p.m. on 11 June 1897 shortly after the enginemen in the winding house had changed shifts. One cage with, by chance, nine miners instead of the usual ten, was ascending the 260 yard shaft when it failed to stop at the top of the pit. The cage, with its unfortunate occupants, was hauled out of the shaft into the head frame tower and, as it struck the cross-members near the top of the tower, the haulage rope became detached from the cage. It plunged down through the shaft in a dreadful free-fall for eight seconds before smashing into the water-filled sump at the pit bottom. Any miners who survived the nightmare fall through the shaft were killed instantly by the crushing weight of the heavy cage roof as its side-supports gave way on impact. The death toll would have been much higher if the next group of ten miners, waiting to ascend at the base of the shaft, had not been ushered away to safety just before the falling cage smashed into the pit bottom. The winding rope on the cage which had just reached the bottom of the pit had become slack as the ill-fated cage at the top was over-wound. So, realising that there might be a problem in the shaft, the waiting miners quickly moved out of danger.

The reasons for the tragedy emerged at the inquest of the nine men. The owners of the mine were cleared of all blame as the winding equipment was found to be in good order, and colliery procedures met all the requirements of the 1887 Act. The accident had occurred because of an inexplicable lapse on the part of the engineman responsible for hauling the men up the shaft. He had simply failed to stop the cage as it reached the top of the pit, a routine operation he had completed thousands of times during many years as a colliery winder. The reasons for his loss of concentration were never explained, though there was some speculation about a 'black-out' or a 'fainting fit', and he escaped prosecution for manslaughter.

The disaster focused attention on the formidable responsibility of the winder who, at that time, operated a fairly primitive haulage system without fail-safe devices. As the lives of the men travelling up and down in the shaft were entirely dependent on his concentration and judgement, a momentary lapse, like the one on 11 June, would have disastrous consequences.

The accident might have been avoided if fail-safe devices had been installed in the head frame tower which could have prevented the cage falling down the shaft after an overwind. For many years safety devices, such as the detaching hook patented by Edward Ormerod in 1865, had been successfully fitted in colliery head frames. The Ormerod Hook was fitted to the top of the cage and, in the event of an overwind, it engaged with a bell-shaped housing in the head frame tower which released the haulage rope and held the cage, preventing it falling back through the shaft. Unfortunately for the nine victims and the winder, colliery proprietors had no legal obligation, under the 1887 Act, to fit such fail-safe devices. It was not until the Coal Mines Act of 1911 that colliery companies were legally bound to provide detaching hooks and other mechanisms to prevent the appalling consequences of an overwind.

The major disasters in the coalfields focused public attention on explosions in particular and often diverted attention away from the dust-related respiratory disease, and the day-to-day accidents that also made coal mining such a dangerous trade. The table below gives a summary of such tragic incidents over an eight-year period in the Llynfi Valley.

Caerau and Coegnant were by far the largest of the collieries, and sinking was taking place at St John's during 1908–9. Rock falls from the roof and the sides of the workings claimed most lives, although haulage activity above and below the surface presented considerable hazards. The average age of fatal accident victims was thirty-two, and 33 per cent of the fatalities were aged twenty-one or under.

FATAL MINING ACCIDENTS IN THE LLYNFI VALLEY, 1902–1909.

	1902			1903			1904			1905			1906			1907			1908			1909			
Colliery	A	B	C	A	B	C	A	B	C	A	B	C	A	B	C	A	B	C	A	B	C	A	B	C	Total
Caerau		1		1			2			2	1	1		1	1		1			2		1	1		15
Coegnant	1			3	1		1	2		3				3			3	1	1	1		3		1	24
Garth										1	1		1	2						1					6
Maesteg Deep	2	1					4												1			2			10
No.9 Level		1			1			1		2							1								6
Oakwood	1						2													1					4
St John's																							1		1

(**A**) – Falls of Rock: 38 fatalities (57 per cent)
(**B**) – Haulage Accidents: 21 (32 per cent)
(**C**) – Surface Accidents: 7 (11 per cent)

Total Fatalities   1902–1909: 66
Annual Totals: 1902: 7, 1903: 6, 1904: 12, 1905: 10, 1906: 7, 1907: 7, 1908: 7, 1909: 10.

Source: Reports of HM Inspectors of Mines 1902–1909

During those eight years, the most serious incident took place at Maesteg Deep Colliery on Monday 14 November 1904, when four men died as a result of a tragic sequence of events that was probably unique in the long history of mining in South Wales. The tragedy was fully recorded in the Report of the Mines' Inspectorate for 1904 and was fully reported in the columns of the *Glamorgan Gazette*.

The colliery was a drift mine in which the men travelled half a mile to the main roadways on a cable-hauled train down a 1:6 gradient. The train could carry seventy-two men in nine carriages, each with eight seats. On that Monday the night shift prepared to descend the drift at 6.30 p.m. The day shift engineman had left at 4.50 p.m. and, because of illness, his replacement for the next shift had not turned up for work. As usual, the engine house had been locked by the day shift engineman at the end of his shift, and the chain securing the throttle valve on the haulage engine had been padlocked. The forty men of the night shift waited in the carriages at the top of the drift and the 'rider', who travelled up and down with the train and other journeys of trams, volunteered to operate the engine and lower the men into the mine. The night shift overman refused the man's offer and, on two occasions, ordered the rider 'not to touch the engine on any account'. After their conversation the overman left the rider and entered the lamp-room. The rider then, inexplicably, squeezed into the locked engine house through the rope-hole, released the brake and set the train in motion. A small number of colliers who had heard the discussion between the overman and the rider, and then saw the rider walk towards the engine house, quickly got off the train as it began to move. It travelled a short distance, and then briefly stopped before running 'down the deep like lightning'. Ten miners, mostly in the front carriages, realising the train was out of control, attempted to jump clear. The ten men incurred serious injuries from which four died in the hours and days that followed. Fortunately the carriages stayed on the rails and came to rest at the bottom of the drift. Apart from an injury to one miner, the men who remained on board were unhurt.

The bizarre behaviour of the rider, who was deemed to have been 'sober' at the time of the tragedy, was fully described at the inquest. After initially releasing the brake he could not 'put on the steam' to regulate the descent of the carriages as the throttle valve was locked. As a result, he lost control of the train which then hurtled down the incline. In desperation, the rider forced the padlock on the chain securing the throttle valve in an attempt to apply steam and check the speed of the carriages. By then, however, the train had miraculously stayed on the track and had come to rest at the bottom of the incline. After leaving the engine house through the rope-hole, the rider disappeared from the scene. He was eventually found by the colliery manager, and gave himself up to the police at 11.00 p.m. He was later found guilty of manslaughter and sentenced to three months in prison. At the inquest the coroner suggested that in future the day engineman should not leave the colliery until the night engineman had arrived and vice versa.

Although the Maesteg Deep tragedy was unusual, it is evident from the above table that fatal accidents were commonplace during the early years of the twentieth century, despite some advances in mining technology, and the passing of important safety legislation. In 1924, there were still eight fatal mining accidents in the Llynfi Valley. As the industry contracted in the 1930s, and as underground safety became a priority, especially after nationalisation, there were fewer fatalities and serious injuries. Nevertheless, long after conditions had improved, the incidence of fatal and serious injuries was still much higher than in other industrial occupations. Two incidents, from the years after nationalisation, served as reminders of that earlier era in the valley when, on average, there was one death every seven weeks in the local collieries. A major tragedy was averted at Caerau Colliery in February 1953 when six miners were rescued after being trapped by a roof fall for fifteen hours and, in October 1954, two men died from the effects of methane poisoning at St John's Colliery.

For many families the saddest consequence of working underground was the high incidence of the prolonged and debilitating illness associated with dust-related diseases. In the years leading up to the First World War over 300 miners died each year in South Wales as a result of dust-related disease, and thousands were disabled by it. Conditions deteriorated further with the introduction of mechanisation in the mines, a process that began in the 1930s and accelerated in the 1950s.

For decades the coal-owners and, to an extent, the government, did not regard dust-related diseases as 'occupational hazards' in the coal industry. The complacent, almost naïve, approach of government agencies to health and safety issues in the mines is reflected in the Report of the Royal Commission on the Mining Industry (1925). In a remarkable summary-paragraph under the sub-heading 'Healthiness of the Occupation' it was noted that: 'Apart from accidents and the industrial diseases special to mining, there is no reason to think that the occupation is physically injurious'. In the same report, dust-related diseases were hardly mentioned and it was noted that: 'In coal mining, the principal industrial disease is nystagmus, which is a troublesome malady of the eyes, that may incapacitate for work for long periods'.

A few years after the report of the Royal Commission, an inquest at Maesteg attracted the attention of the national press as questions were raised about the need to schedule coal miners' silicosis as an industrial disease. The Government's Mines Department, the Mines Inspectorate, the South Wales Coal-Owners' Association and the South Wales Miners' Federation were all represented at the inquest, and the proceedings were fully reported in *The Times* of 30 August 1928. The report allows a glimpse of prevailing attitudes to dust-related disease during the late 1920s. The inquest was on a local collier who had been driving hard headings at one of North's collieries. When the miner first saw his local doctor, phthisis or tuberculosis was diagnosed; some time later the local general practitioner was of the opinion that the collier's illness was consistent with silicosis, which was not a 'scheduled' coal miners' disease under the terms of the Workmens' Compensation Acts. The doctor also commented that although miners' respiratory problems were usually diagnosed as tuberculosis or chronic bronchitis, 'there was more silicosis about than people imagined'. Specialist opinion was provided by the senior pathologist at Cardiff Royal Infirmary who certified the cause of death as acute pneumonia following silicosis, adding a rider that silicosis would reduce the chance of recovery from pneumonia. The jury returned a verdict of 'death from acute pneumonia following silicosis'.

Thus in the late 1920s, although the miners' unions had long been insisting that the disabling pulmonary diseases that afflicted thousands of miners were related to working conditions, the illnesses were usually diagnosed as tuberculosis, chronic bronchitis and pneumonia, which were not scheduled industrial diseases under the Workmens' Compensation Acts. Coal miners' silicosis, however, was scheduled in 1934 although the payment of compensation was delayed until 1937 due to legal challenges by the coal-owners. It was not until 1942, after six years of 'careful scientific investigation' among the South Wales miners, and after over a century of large-scale mining in South Wales, that all dust-related mining diseases, collectively called 'pneumoconiosis', were acknowledged as hazardous diseases by the Industrial Pulmonary Disease Committee of the General Medical Council. As a result, mineworkers suffering from all forms of dust-related illness could, at long last, look forward to some form of compensation. However the compensation scheme devised after the announcement by the British Medical Council created further problems for many miners. The compensation regulations introduced in 1943 stipulated that although all colliers certified with pneumoconiosis would receive a lump sum or a weekly payment in compensation, they would also be suspended from their employment in the mining industry. As a consequence, due to the shortage of suitable light industrial work in the valleys of South Wales, many disabled miners faced long-term unemployment and were financially worse off after their suspension. In 1951 however, in the face of acute manpower shortages, the NUM and the NCB agreed to re-employ some workers with lower levels of disability under the Re-employment Scheme.

Although 'dust-management' improved in the collieries after the Second World War and there was better medical screening and health care, dust-related disease was still an occupational hazard, and the legacy of earlier working conditions remained. As late as the 1970s significant numbers of relatively young local miners were severely disabled by dust-related disease. Some were house-bound and dependent on their families, for others the daily routine was limited to a breathless but determined walk in the local district. More recently, in the late 1990s, elderly former miners with chronic bronchitis and emphysema were still fighting for some form of compensation for the damage to their health that had resulted from years of work in dusty conditions.

The 1925 report noted above did at least emphasise the seriousness of nystagmus, the disabling eye condition. The disease often resulted when colliers worked in poorly-lit conditions over long periods. Some concern was expressed in the report about the high incidence of nystagmus during the early 1920s and recommendations were made regarding the increased provision of electric lighting, and the adoption of flame safety lamps with greater candle-power.

The hazards facing coal miners, certainly before the Second World War, can be placed in perspective through comparisons with other industries. In the 1925 Report of the Royal Commission, it was noted that, in terms of fatal accidents, only employment in 'shipping' (presumably the Merchant Navy) was (marginally) more dangerous than working underground. Also, as far as fatal accidents were concerned, a coal miner's occupation was eight times more dangerous than a factory worker's. In terms of non-fatal accidents, coal mining was by far the most dangerous occupation in Britain.

CHAPTER NINE

MASTERS AND MEN

INDUSTRIAL DISPUTES IN THE LLYNFI VALLEY COAL INDUSTRY

From the early years of the coal industry, industrial unrest inevitably flared up from time to time as mining companies sought maximum returns for shareholders and the workforce toiled in conditions that were difficult and dangerous. In the Llynfi Valley the earliest disputes were local affairs in support of pay claims or in protest at reductions in wage rates. By the end of the nineteenth century, mineworkers were well organised in trade unions and began to effectively challenge the coal-owners at regional and national level. In the early twentieth century the quest for trade union solidarity added a further dimension to industrial disputes as the South Wales Miners' Federation attempted to ensure membership of that trade union was universal. During the latter part of the twentieth century, after nationalisation, the major disputes developed into nationwide 'set-piece' conflicts between the miners and successive Conservative governments.

In the earliest phase of mining the Llynfi Valley colliers were employed by the iron companies. Their position, when in dispute with the ironmasters, was relatively weak as they were not effectively organised and strike leaders could be arrested for 'deserting their work'. In addition, reserves of coal were often stock-piled at the ironworks and striking colliers rarely had the support of fellow workers at the furnaces, forges and mills.

The earliest industrial dispute in the valley was probably the colliers' strike at the Maesteg Ironworks in January 1835. From a detailed report in *The Cambrian*, the dispute arose after wage increases, introduced by the company early in 1834 when iron prices were high, were withdrawn in December of that year after a fall in iron prices. At first the colliers accepted the reduction, but, some days later, they decided to strike in protest. In reply, the iron company 'made up their minds to stop the works, and they accordingly allowed the furnaces to go out'. Warrants were obtained by the company against five of the 'ringleaders' who were brought before the Bridgend magistrates. The rather dramatic intervention in the crowded courtroom of Robert Smith, the 'leading partner at the works', ensured a reprimand rather than a conviction for the strike leaders, and a swift return to work.

Significantly, the Bridgend magistrates played a key role in the 1835 dispute, and in the late 1830s when the Chartists were advocating democratic reforms, some local Justices of the Peace were keen to limit the spread of such 'fallacious and dangerous doctrines'. The letters of James Bicheno JP, of Ty-Maen, South Cornelly, in the Bute Estate Collection at the National Library of Wales, give an insight into the methods employed in the Llynfi Valley to check the spread of Chartism and preserve the status quo. During 1840, after the Chartist unrest in the western valleys of Monmouthshire, Bicheno sent reports to the Marquess of Bute (the Lord Lieutenant of Glamorgan), regarding the threat of Chartism in the Llynfi Valley. In a letter early in November he reports in some detail on the movements of a 'delegate from Blackwood [Mon.]' who had visited Maesteg. He then informs the marquess that Daniel Samuels from Abersychan in Monmouthshire had been discharged by the Cambrian Co. for 'using seditious language'. In the same letter Bicheno reports that the managers at the Maesteg Works had been instructed to discharge 'any man who gives countenance to the Chartists'. In another letter, in December 1840, he notes that 'a Chartist delegate' had visited Maesteg on three or four occasions, leaving literature for 'certain workmen' in the public house of Joan Roderick. He regretted that no evidence could be found. Despite the occasional visitors, James Bicheno was confident that the Chartist movement would not take hold in the Llynfi Valley; he summarised his findings thus:

> I find much satisfaction in stating that Chartism does not appear to make progress at Maesteg, and I trust, with proper vigilance and vigour we will be able to suppress it altogether.

During the late 1830s and early 1840s James Bicheno and his fellow magistrates in Bridgend had to contend with the emergence of a large industrial population in what was a country district with a rural system of local government. The magistrates, mainly local clergymen and landowners, administered justice as they had done for decades, but, by the 1830s, they were also major shareholders in many of the new industries in the locality. As, at that time, industrial disputes were often 'settled' by the local Bench, conflict was inevitable, as the magistrates often had an interest in the companies that were challenged by strike action.

During the Maesteg colliers' strike of 1835 a fairly compliant workforce and the timely intervention of Robert Smith of the Maesteg Works had ensured that the ambivalent role of the magistrates was not challenged in any way. Ten years later, in 1845, the role of the Bench during local industrial disputes was brought into sharp focus, and was drawn to the attention of the Marquess of Bute and the Home Secretary, Sir James Graham.

During the summer of 1845 the colliers employed at the small Coed-y-Garth Colliery in Maesteg, which was owned by Messrs Malins and Rawlinson, were in dispute with the company over the irregular pattern of payment at the mine. The miners alleged that Malins & Co., who paid the workforce at intervals of seven to nine weeks, often paid the men for just five weeks' work when the wages for nine were due. Also the men and their families had no choice but to spend their wages in the company's truck shop. Over a number of months the company had failed to honour promises to pay wages in full, so the miners lost patience and went on strike. As was the case in 1835, warrants were issued for the 'ringleaders' and seven men were arrested for 'quitting the service of Messrs Malins & Co. without giving the usual notice'. There the similarity with the earlier dispute ends as the miners' cause was taken up by a Morgan Davies of 'Llangynwyd Village', an articulate spokesman for the strikers. In a remarkable letter to the Marquess of Bute, Davies complained in no uncertain terms about the harsh treatment of the arrested men and the biased nature of the Bridgend Bench. His observations give an insight into the conflicts between an essentially eighteenth-century system of local administration and a rapidly expanding industrial population.

Davies stated the miners' case lucidly, arguing that if Malins & Co. did not honour their agreement to pay the men at regular intervals, why should the miners honour their contract to give 'the usual notice'? He also complained that the arrested men were 'handcuffed like Slaves of America' and that the 'Head of the family of Justices' on the Bench was a partner of Malins & Co. in a local railway venture. The 'family' referred to was made up of the three presiding magistrates: the Revd Robert Knight (the 'Head of the Family') and his sons-in-law Revd H.L. Blosse and William Llewellyn.

The Marquess of Bute took Davies's letter very seriously and the police officer in charge at Bridgend, Superintendent Corr, had to justify his treatment of the prisoners to the Home Secretary. In a letter to Sir James Graham, Corr recalled an incident two years earlier when a prisoner 'was rescued and carried away in triumph' after the superintendent and two constables were 'furiously assaulted in the streets of Bridgend by a mob composed chiefly of miners and colliers'. In view of that incident, Corr explained that it was necessary to handcuff the prisoners on the journey to Bridgend 'as they were guarded by two constables only, through a wild and mountainous country in the presence of their excited fellow workmen'. Under the circumstances, with just three constables, a large area to police and a hostile workforce to contend with, the superintendent informed Sir James Graham that the 'whole transaction was efficiently executed without injury to a single individual'.

After being initially sentenced to one month's hard labour, the arrested men were then released and, apparently, the dispute ended. After the Coed-y-Garth strike the local magistrates were no longer directly involved in the settlement of industrial disputes in the district. From the mid-1840s to the 1860s local disagreements were thus mainly internal affairs between a large but poorly organised workforce, and determined industrialists.

Such a dispute occurred in 1847 when a major strike by the colliers employed by the Llynvi Iron Co. was provoked by a 20 per cent wage cut. As there were stockpiles of coal at the works and the ironworkers continued to produce metal, the company remained in a strong position and the strike was ineffective. When the colliers' grievances were the same as the ironworkers, strikes were more prolonged yet rarely more effective. In 1853, for example, there was an unsuccessful ten-week protest by colliers and ironworkers against the re-introduction of the truck system by the Llynvi Vale Iron Co.

From press reports in the 1860s there is some evidence of trade union activity in the valley. For instance, at the inquest on the miners killed by the Gin Pit explosion which was held in January 1864, *The Cambrian* reported that a 'Mr D. Stevenson, one of the Council of the National Association of Miners, with Mr J.M. Barrett, solicitor, Leeds, attended to watch the proceedings on behalf of the association'.

By the early 1870s many miners in the Maesteg area belonged to the short-lived, Lancashire-based, Amalgamated Association of Miners (AAM) led by Thomas Halliday. Open-air union meetings were held on the 'Garn Top', presumably where Pen-y-Garn Terrace is now located. One of the first mass-meetings was held in June 1872. During the gathering a Mr Henry Thomas, miners' agent, said that, a few months earlier, when he had visited Maesteg, 'few had joined the union'; he then noted that, 'now the members here are numbered in hundreds, and perhaps thousands'. Three months later, on 19 September, a substantial temporary platform was erected on the 'Garn Top' and Thomas Halliday addressed 'a strong muster of men – from 1,200 to 1,500'.

Although Henry Thomas had speculated that there were 'perhaps thousands' of union members in the Maesteg district, there were in fact 899 registered members in the Maesteg branch of the Amalgamated Association of Miners in September 1872. The figure was included in a report in *The Cambrian* of a conference held by the AAM in Walsall. Membership of the AAM had increased spectacularly from 6,500 in October 1869 to 70,536 by October 1872, and it is probable that well over half the miners in the Maesteg district were recruited by the AAM during 1871–2.

During a brief period of prosperity in the coal and iron industries in the early 1870s, the miners sought better wages. The coal-owners and ironmasters refused to meet the colliers' demands and a coalfield strike ensued at the end of 1872. At that time almost all the Llynfi Valley miners were employed by the Llynvi, Tondu & Ogmore Coal & Iron Co. As noted in an earlier chapter, the chairman of the company, Alexander Brogden, preferred to lead his own negotiations with his workers, free from the influence of the other coal-owners and ironmasters in South Wales. Alexander Brogden brought the strike to an end in the Llynfi Valley when he acted unilaterally and settled with the men in the middle of February 1873. He then continued the company system of pay reviews for the workforce every three months.

The first review of 1874 resulted in an increase for the miners but, by the time of the next review, in April, the company, like the other iron-making enterprises in South Wales, sought wage reductions as the price of iron had decreased sharply. In May, on the recommendation of the miners' leader, Thomas Halliday, a 10 per cent reduction was accepted by the men. As iron prices continued to fall and the Llynfi company wanted to reduce wages further, there were a number of local stoppages in 1875 and a nine-week dispute at the Dyffryn Pit which ended in April 1877.

After the industrial unrest in South Wales during the period 1873–5, the Sliding Scale was introduced in the latter year. An increase of 1s on the price of coal would result in a wage rise of 7½ per cent. Although there was at least a coalfield-based negotiating structure in place after 1875, with less than a third of the South Wales miners in trade unions, and Halliday's Amalgamated Association of Miners in decline, the Sliding Scale was not universally applied. There is no evidence that the system was practised in the Llynfi Valley in the late 1870s. Local considerations prevailed and the three month review arrangement continued until the demise of the Llynvi Coal & Iron Co. in January 1878.

During the early 1880s, however, the old bargaining arrangements on a local scale began to be replaced by negotiations at regional and national level. In January 1882 a new era of trade unionism commenced in the Llynfi Valley when William Abraham (Mabon), the leader of the Cambrian Miners' Association, addressed a mass meeting of 600 colliers at the new town hall in Maesteg. At the meeting the Llynfi Valley miners resolved to support the Sliding Scale Committee and form a 'united front' with other coalfield districts. Mabon, a moderate with a dislike of confrontation, was vice-chairman of the joint committee of coal-owners and trade unionists that operated the Sliding Scale Agreement. Although union membership was far from universal and there were other miners' unions, the 1882 meeting marked the beginning of the transition from ineffective local bargaining to modern trade unionism for the Llynfi Valley colliers.

The industrial unrest of the mid-1870s in South Wales was followed by a period of relative peace in the coalfield. From this time of limited confrontation came the concession of a day's holiday each month, granted in 1888 and named after the leader of the Cambrian Miners' Association. In 1890, for example, miners in North's collieries worked a six day week, Sundays and the first Monday in each month (Mabon's Day) were the only days of rest.

During the 1890s there were frequent local disputes over wage rates at the coal face. As noted above there was a lengthy stoppage at the new Caerau Colliery over coal-cutting rates. The Caerau dispute is remarkably well documented in the archive of South Wales Coal-Owners' Association at the National Library of Wales, and gives some indication of the pattern of industrial relations in the coalfield in the 1890s. The stoppage, which began on 1 April 1894 and ended in February 1896, was essentially the result of a pay-rate anomaly at the neighbouring Coegnant Colliery. The coal-cutting rate at Coegnant for the seam known locally as the *Maesteg Nine Feet* seam was 1s 10d per ton and had been set some years earlier, before North's had taken over the colliery. When North's opened the new Caerau Colliery, the vein of coal that the colliers regarded as the continuation of the *Maesteg Nine Feet* seam from Coegnant, was referred to by North's as the *Six Feet* seam and a rate of 1s. 5d per ton was set. This was the same rate as the *Six Feet* seam in the Ogmore, Garw and Rhondda Valleys.

The Caerau men were determined to demonstrate that they did not 'bind themselves to accept Rhondda prices in Maesteg', and, after weeks of argument with North's Navigation over the identity of the seam, the 130 or so Caerau miners involved in the dispute rejected arbitration, despite the efforts of the Cambrian Miners' Association, and went on strike for parity with the Coegnant rate. Although it was a small-scale dispute it presented considerable problems for the Coal-Owners' Association. If the Caerau rate were increased to the Coegnant figure, miners in other collieries working the *Six Feet* seam could seek the same benefits. Also, during the dispute, many of the Caerau strikers left the area temporarily and found work in other pits affiliated to the Coal-Owners' Association. A great deal of time and energy was expended by the association in 'tracking down' and discharging Caerau colliers from mines across South Wales.

On 20 June 1894 the miners at Garth and other collieries in the valley joined a major demonstration in Maesteg in support of the strike. A large group of colliers assembled at the town hall, marched in protest to the Caerau pits, and then returned to the town centre. During the march a small number of Caerau workers, who were not prepared to support the dispute, were forcibly taken from their homes, dressed in white shirts and paraded around the town. Because of the intimidation of the Caerau workers, fifteen strike supporters were arrested during the demonstration and committed for trial.

The Caerau strikers, led by David Beynon, were able to hold out against the might of the Coal-Owners' Association as they received strike pay from subscriptions made by other Llynfi Valley miners. By May 1895, over a year after the start of the strike, the directors of North's were concerned that work on their considerable investment at the Caerau pits, one of the largest developments in the coalfield, was almost at a standstill. Negotiations broke down again in August 1895, and, in September, John Boyd-Harvey, the general manager of North's, made new attempts to end the strike. As a consequence of Boyd-Harvey's initiatives, the nature of the dispute changed dramatically. With the eventual support of the Coal-Owners' Association, he closed Coegnant Colliery on 1 November 1895 with the result that over 600 miners were without work. What had been a relatively small-scale strike involving a small number of miners who could receive some strike pay, suddenly became a major dispute with a large number of men and their families facing hardship and unemployment. By January 1896 there was considerable distress in the Llynfi Valley as a result of the closure of Coegnant and appeals for help were made. Early in February 1896 Boyd-Harvey presented a compromise cutting rate to the Caerau miners and, at the same time, threatened to close Park-Slip Colliery in Aberkenfig and No.9 in Maesteg if the dispute continued. The new rate was agreed by the miners' representative, John Thomas (miners' agent), and the strike ended on 11 February 1896.

The Caerau miners had been on strike for twenty-two months, and the Coegnant men had been 'locked-out' for eighty-three working days. Typically for the time, the Caerau strike had depended on local solidarity rather than organised union support, and the Coal-Owners' Association had demonstrated its authority by controlling the movement of striking miners and by compensating North's for losses incurred during the dispute.

The first of a series of regional and national disputes with the South Wales coal-owners, which would continue into the 1920s, occurred with the 'great lock-out' of 1898. During the 1890s the coal industry was expanding rapidly, workforces were increasing and there was growing pressure among the miners for reform of the pay structure and the removal of the strait-jacket of the Sliding Scale. In September 1897 the miners' leaders gave the owners six month's notice that the Sliding Scale should be terminated and replaced by a 10 per cent wage increase and a minimum wage. At the end of March 1898 the South Wales coal-owners replied and defied the miners with a lock-out. As a result, 2,800 miners and their families in the valley were faced with a long struggle for survival.

The story of the dispute and the distress it brought to the Llynfi Valley can be traced via the columns of the *Glamorgan Gazette* during the summer of 1898. As North's was affiliated to the Coal-Owners' Association, all the company's workers were involved in the dispute. The owners of Garth and Oakwood collieries were not affiliated so local arrangements were made with the workforce. In March at Oakwood the men accepted a substantial offer from their employers and the mine continued in production. The Garth miners refused their employer's initial offer and decided to join the struggle along with North's colliers.

By the end of April 1898 the effects of the dispute were beginning to affect all aspects of life in the valley. There was a shortage of house coal in the district, and it was reported that 'the old colliery tops are being tumbled over and ransacked to obtain a little of the necessary fuel'. At the same time old levels were unofficially re-opened. A Relief Committee was set up in Maesteg at the beginning of May, and shortly afterwards there were 'hundreds at the Town Hall to receive the [weekly] pittance of Relief Fund being distributed'. At about the same time the first 'soup kitchen' was opened at Caerau which provided meals for 200 needy children. The first soup kitchen in Maesteg was set up at the beginning of June at the Central Infants' School. It was the result of an initiative by the teaching staff at the school, and provided breakfasts and afternoon meals for over 200 children during the dispute.

The Garth miners held out until August when they accepted a 10 per cent wage increase and returned to work. The Coal-Owners' Association had no intention of conceding any ground to the miners and, in early September, after a twenty-two week struggle, the workforce reluctantly returned to North's pits in the valley. On the face of it the dispute was a disaster for the miners and their families and, to add insult to injury, the coal-owners abolished the concession of 'Mabon's Day' after the dispute. Yet, in many ways, the 1898 lock-out was a turning point for the colliers; the South Wales Miners' Federation (SWMF) was formed a month after the dispute ended, and there was a new determination among the workforce to form a united front against the might of the coal-owners.

The Maesteg district became a stronghold of the new union. In September 1906 the *Western Mail* reported disturbances in the Llynfi Valley as attempts were made to increase union membership in the area, a trend that would lead to further confrontation over union membership in the district in later years.

As membership of the SWMF increased, a number of able union leaders with growing political influence emerged in the coalfield districts. In the Maesteg area, Vernon Hartshorn, a native of Pontywaun near Risca in Monmouthshire, became the miners' agent in 1905, and was elected chairman of the Maesteg Urban District Council in 1908.

During his early years as the local miners' agent, Vernon Hartshorn would have been involved with the day-to-day disputes that were part and parcel of the colliery routine. Brief glimpses of typical disputes at North's collieries can be obtained from entries in the Coegnant Colliery Disputes' Book for 1911 conserved at University College, Swansea.

Before the introduction of the minimum wage, coal-cutting rates were set by the company in agreement with the miners' representatives, led locally by Vernon Hartshorn. Also 'quality control' standards at the coal face were strictly enforced by the colliery management. Disputes inevitably arose when, because of local variations along the coal seams, it was difficult, often impossible, to obtain a 'living wage' by applying the standard cutting rates. Also colliers, through their representatives, sometimes challenged the management after they had been dismissed, or suspended, for breaking the rigidly applied colliery rules that prohibited filling trams by the shovel, or filling trams with waste material.

In January 1911 for example, two colliers were suspended for 'sending out a dirty tram'. They were reinstated a week later after presenting a written apology to the manager, and forfeiting the filled tram. In the same month a collier was suspended for a week for 'filling [a tram] with the shovel' rather than by hand or with a curling box.

The most serious disputes related to the problem of applying fixed cutting rates for piece-work in 'abnormal places' where mining conditions could change dramatically over a few metres. From time to time colliers would argue that although hours would be spent at the coal face, output was often low due to conditions which were outside their control (for example, poor quality coal, shortage of trams and small-scale faults or 'jumps in the coal'). One extract from the disputes book graphically illustrates the problems encountered by miners shackled by fixed cutting rates in difficult mining areas:

> The width of the face is about 14 yards and for half the distance the coal is very soft. A lot of rubbish had to be shifted twice before it could be taken out. The place is also very warm and dusty owing to bad ventilation, or no ventilation at all. The men have to work in a cloud of dust all day.

Miners working in a better district with the same cutting rates would inevitably earn much higher wages. Often the problem was resolved by the manager and colliers re-negotiating a fair rate for the job. On other occasions the miners' representative at the colliery would negotiate on the colliers' behalf. The more complicated disagreements recorded in the Coegnant Disputes' Books were simply marked 'referred to Hartshorn' or 'query to Hartshorn'.

Peaceful Persuasion:
or, Strengthening the numbers of the Federation at Maesteg.

Western Mail cartoon after disturbances over union membership in the Llynfi Valley, September 1906.

A former miner and colliery check-weigher, Vernon Hartshorn became a prominent figure in the SWMF and the Labour Party during the years before the First World War, and was a major influence on industrial relations in the coalfield. He successfully charted a middle course between the cautious 'Old Guard' of the Mabon era and the much more radical, militant, syndicalist miners' leaders. His balanced approach was well-received by the Llynfi Valley miners, and such was his growing reputation as a leader and a negotiator that it was to the Maesteg District, (together with the Rhondda No.1 and Aberdare Districts), that the rest of the coalfield looked for leadership.

During the First World War Hartshorn was a key member of the Coal Controller's Advisory Council and the Coal Trade Organising Committee; he was awarded the OBE for his wartime service to the coal industry. After being returned unopposed as the first MP for the new Ogmore Constituency in 1918, he had a distinguished parliamentary career. Vernon Hartshorn was the first former Welsh miner to achieve Cabinet rank: he was Post-Master General in the first-ever Labour government of 1924 and Lord Privy Seal when Labour returned to power in 1929. Hartshorn was also an influential member of the Simon Commission that reported on constitutional reform in India in 1930.

As a union official and then as the local MP, Vernon Hartshorn supported the Maesteg miners during the major strikes and lock-outs of the period 1910–27. In the former year, during the lock-out and rioting at the Rhondda Valley collieries, there was a short-lived strike in the Maesteg area; the miners employed by North's came out on strike at the beginning of November in support of the traffic-men at the local pits who were in dispute with the company. During March–April 1912 there was a partially successful national strike in support of a minimum wage for miners. It was during the 1912 dispute that Hartshorn became nationally known as a prominent trade union leader. In October 1911 he had been elected to the Executive of the Miners' Federation of Great Britain, and his speeches on the minimum wage issue frequently attracted the attention of the national press during the winter of 1911–12. Hartshorn thus played a key role in the dispute that eventually led to the passing of the Mines (Minimum Wage) Act of 1912.

In November 1916, the government took control of the South Wales collieries under the Defence of the Realm Act, and the pits remained under state control until 1921. The direct involvement of the government in the coal industry ensured relatively high wages and better working conditions for the South Wales miners. Early in 1921 the coal-owners resumed control of the collieries, and the government refused to accept the proposals of the Sankey Commission which recommended the nationalisation of the mines. Because the coal-owners sought to reduce production costs when the miners wanted to maintain the reasonable gains made during the years of government control, a clash was inevitable. There was a national strike from March to July 1921 and once again miners and their families had to endure acute poverty and hardship. The coal-owners were again successful and there were wage reductions in the months that followed.

As international markets became more competitive, and the government avoided intervention, the coal-owners' response was to further reduce wages and increase working hours. As a result, the Llynfi Valley district, like all the South Wales mining communities, endured the unsuccessful seven-month dispute of 1926 and the short-lived General Strike of that year.

During the 1926 dispute, as in previous strikes and lock-outs, the local community was 'mobilised' in support of the miners. For example, meals were provided for children and boot-repairing depots were set up as the colliery lodges, together with local churches and chapels, attempted to alleviate the hardships experienced by colliers and their families. Across the country, fund-raising events were organised, donations were made in support of the strikers, and local miners' choirs took part in fund-raising concerts all over Britain.

The records of the Maesteg District Distress Fund, in the South Wales Coalfield Collection at University College, Swansea, give an insight into the way local people worked together to support the miners during the prolonged dispute. For example, at the end of June 1926 the Distress Fund Committee decided to set up canteens to provide one meal a day for the single men involved in the dispute. The canteens, with secretaries, were set up at Caerau Institute, Salem Chapel, Nantyffyllon, the Co-op building in Maesteg, Libanus Chapel in Garth, and

The Maesteg Miners' Septet at Islington during the 1926 strike. The septet was one of the official fund-raising choirs engaged by the influential London-based Women's Committee for the Relief of Miners' Wives and Children.

Ainon Chapel, Pontrhydycyff. Initially the daily meal consisted of bread, cheese and tea, although cooked meals were provided in later weeks. By the end of the dispute almost 90,000 meals had been served in the canteens.

Towards the end of the dispute, in October 1926, Maesteg miners were involved in one of the most serious outbreaks of violence during the strike when they clashed with police at Glyncymer Colliery in nearby Cymer Afan. Many of the Glyncymer miners had decided to return to work, and a large number of Llynfi Valley colliers gathered near the mine in an attempt to persuade the returning miners to rejoin the struggle with the coal-owners. When police reinforcements arrived at the scene by motor-coach, stones were thrown by the strikers. The police responded with a baton-charge which dispersed the crowd; forty-seven people were injured and twenty-four strikers were arrested.

Tensions between the coal-owners and the miners re-surfaced in the Maesteg district in 1927 during a drive by the SWMF against non-unionism in the Llynfi Valley. In May an ultimatum to join the SWMF was given to 100 local members of The South Wales & Monmouthshire Colliery Enginemen, Boilermen & Craftsmen's Association. When fifty refused to join, 6,000 miners in the district went on strike. Some days later, after local demonstrations by thousands of miners, the strike ended when the fifty members of the craftsmen's association agreed to join the SWMF.

The coal-owners obviously wanted to discourage the establishment of a single union in the coalfield and an example was made of the Maesteg miners. When the men returned to work after the strike they were locked out by North's as, according to the company, 'work was not available'. The lock-out lasted a week and prompted a strong response from Vernon Hartshorn which was well publicised via the letters page of the *Western Mail*. Hartshorn, once described as the 'statesman of the coal industry' by Lloyd George, saw the coal-owners' self-interest as a negative force in a coalfield that was facing foreign competition and consequent unemployment. He regretted the government's failure to intervene and implement the recommendations of the Sankey Commission, and believed that a single union would promote better industrial relations in the longer term. Although Vernon Hartshorn was generally regarded as a moderate who viewed strike action as a last resort, he could be confrontational over the issue of non-unionism. He was always ready to organise strike action to achieve 100 per cent local membership of the SWMF, and his militant approach was one of the main reasons why the Maesteg district had a reputation for forcefully challenging non-unionism in the collieries.

Although the majority of the Maesteg miners valued Hartshorn's support and his good counsel, as far as the small but significant Maesteg branch of the Communist Party was concerned, Vernon Hartshorn had become more of an 'establishment figure' during the First World War. His more moderate approach sometimes frustrated the local Communist Party members who were active in the district during the 1920s. They were also a little taken aback by his rather 'aristocratic tastes' which also surprised Shapurji Saklatvala, the Indian-born Communist MP for Battersea. Saklatvala was one of Hartshorn's chief critics, especially after the MP for Ogmore had joined the Simon Commission. During a meeting at Blaengarw in 1928, for example, Shapurji Saklatvala was particularly critical of the local MP. Hartshorn was also in favour of the expulsion of members of the Communist Party from the Labour Party and, such was the extent of the rift between the MP and the local Communists in the mid-1920s, Hartshorn once called the police to evict Communist Party members from a meeting of the Ogmore Labour Party in Bridgend. However, despite the conflicts and the arguments, 'the left wing' of the local Labour Party and the Llynfi Valley Communists acknowledged that the great majority of the miners in Maesteg were 'solid for Hartshorn'.

After serving the Maesteg district for twenty-six years, Vernon Hartshorn died suddenly at his home in Salisbury Road on 13 March 1931, aged fifty-nine. Twenty thousand people gathered in Maesteg to pay their respects at the funeral; the *Glamorgan Gazette* reported that: 'along the three-mile route to the churchyard [at Llangynwyd], the cortege passed through densely lined crowds of sympathisers'. Among the mourners were the Home Secretary, J.R. Clynes, and Clement Attlee, who represented the Cabinet, together with numerous representatives of local government agencies, the trade unions and the coal-owners. Unlike other prominent personalities associated with the industrial development of the Llynfi Valley, men such as Sir John Bowring, Colonel John North and Sir Alfred Jones, Vernon Hartshorn lived among his friends and constituents in Maesteg and played an active role in the community as miners' agent, local councillor and MP.

The year of Vernon Hartshorn's death, 1931, also marked the low point of the Depression years in the Maesteg district. In the Llynfi Valley during 1930-1, 2,560 miners lost their jobs (52 per cent of the workforce) and poverty and unemployment reached alarming levels. Large-scale migration from the district was another consequence of the rapid decline of the coal industry. The era of large workforces, massive membership of the SWMF and continual, large-scale conflict with the coal-owners was over. The industrial disputes of the 1930s and early 1940s would be smaller-scale affairs that were usually prompted by local working conditions. Two significant exceptions were the 'Boys' Strikes' of the early 1940s and the short-lived 'Porter Award dispute' of 1944.

During the early years of the Second World War there was growing dissatisfaction among the boys (or colliers' assistants) in the South Wales area about their levels of pay, methods of payment and their general working conditions. Further frustration resulted locally when the lads made comparisons with their peers who earned good wages at the Royal Ordnance Factory at Bridgend. Due to the government's wartime 'Essential Work Order' the young miners had no option but to remain in the pits. In the Maesteg district the boys were also unhappy over a system of 'informal' payments known as 'Trumps'. The boys received the trumps from the colliers they worked for. The lads argued that they found it difficult to collect their trumps as they might work for four or five colliers during the week. They wanted to collect their payments at the beginning of the week.

Against this background of growing unrest among the colliers' assistants, a series of uncoordinated strikes criss-crossed the coalfield during 1942 as the young colliers, without organisation or effective leadership, attempted to improve their wages and working conditions. One unsuccessful 'chain-reaction' by the boys began in the western part of the coalfield, then spread to the Kenfig Hill district before reaching pits in the Garw and the Llynfi Valleys.

Immediately after the Second World War trade unionism in the mines went through a process of rapid change. In 1945 the South Wales Miners' Federation was replaced by the National Union of Mineworkers (NUM) and on 1 January 1947 the coal mines were nationalised. At the same time, the introduction of the Welfare State and the National Health Service also affected the traditional role of the miners' union in the coalfield communities. Up to 1945 the colliery lodges of the SWMF had influenced many aspects of community life as they supported their members and their families over housing provision, health care and a range of other social issues. The lodges, for example, had largely funded the Maesteg General Hospital for more than thirty years from its beginnings during the First World War until the advent of the National Health Service. After World War II, however, the lodges played a less influential role as new national and local agencies provided a range of services for the coalfield communities.

The relationship between 'masters and men' became an association between 'management and men' with the nationalisation of the mines. Vesting Day, 1 January 1947, was formally marked in the Llynfi Valley with ceremonies at the local collieries. At Coegnant, for example, a plaque was unveiled to mark the takeover of the mine by the National Coal Board, the blue 'Vesting Flag' was unfurled, speeches were made and hymns were sung at the pit head. All the speakers emphasised the need for cooperation between the workforce and the new board, and many of the speakers specifically referred to the bright future ahead for the younger generation of miners and the debt the young men owed to those who had campaigned for nationalisation for decades.

Apart from the inevitable local disputes at the collieries and some regional stoppages, there was an absence of large-scale conflict in the coalfields for many years after nationalisation. However by the early 1970s attitudes hardened as the NUM successfully challenged the National Coal Board (and the Conservative government) with a series of national strikes in January–February 1972 and in February 1974. The latter strike was a major reason for the hung Parliament and the failure of the Conservatives to form a government after the General Election of February 1974. Both strikes were over wage increases and, from the miners' point of view, they were the most successful industrial disputes in well over a century of trade unionism in the coal industry.

The election of a Conservative government in 1979 heralded a new approach to the viability of the traditional heavy industries in Britain, and an era of conflict in the coalfields. The new administration sought to limit the power of the NUM and implement a major programme of colliery closures across the country as socio-economic considerations gave way to a quest for profitability driven by purely market forces. The process began in February 1981 when the National Coal Board announced a limited closure programme that involved Coegnant Colliery. Shortly after the announcement, the Coegnant men walked out on an unofficial strike that sparked similar protests in other areas affected by closures. A few days later, in response to the unofficial strikes which began at Coegnant, the government changed tactics and withdrew the planned closure programme, for a time at least. At the time of the dispute the main reasons given by the Coal Board for the proposed closure of Coegnant were the contracting market for coking coal due to falling demand from the British Steel Corporation, and the unacceptably high ash content in the coking coal produced at a recently opened new face.

In reality the closure programme went ahead through the Colliery Review Procedure and, nine months after the unofficial strike, the closure of Coegnant was announced in early November. This time the closure was due to geological problems at the mine.

The relatively small programme of closures announced in February 1981 was just the beginning of the major conflict over pit closures and the future of the coal industry that led to the year-long national dispute of 1984–5. After the failures of the 1970s, the Conservative government was determined not to concede any ground to the miners and, after twelve months, the colliers had no alternative but to face the prospect of large-scale pit closures and make an organised return to work. For the Llynfi Valley colliers and their families involved in the strike, the hardship and the frustration endured in 1984–5 were comparable in many ways to the experience of generations of miners during the long disputes with the coal-owners in a different era of conflict. The dispute was the longest major strike in the Llynfi district and, as it was followed by the demise of the British coal industry, it was also the last. The year 1985 thus marked the end of a long series of industrial disputes in the Llynfi Valley collieries that began with the strike at the Maesteg Ironworks in 1835.

CHAPTER TEN

THE TYPES OF COAL PRODUCED IN THE LLYNFI VALLEY

Within the relatively small area of the upper Llynfi Valley the coals produced were characterised by their quality and their suitability for a range of markets. As outlined in an earlier chapter, the initial development of the district had occurred because coal suitable for converting into blast furnace coke could be cheaply mined on or near the surface. By the 1860s the qualities of local coal for steam raising were also recognised. Gold medals were awarded to Llynfi Valley coal producers for 'Superiority of Smokeless Steam Coal' at international exhibitions in France and the Netherlands in 1868 and 1869. By the early 1870s it was realised that the untapped reserves under Mynydd Caerau, at the head of the valley, contained seams of even better quality steam coal; it was the development of those resources that transformed the district in the Edwardian period. The coals mined south of the Caerau and Coegnant steam coal pits were slightly more bituminous and were suited to general steam raising, coke making and the house coal market.

During the heyday of the South Wales coal trade, the valley thus served four broad market areas. High-quality steam coal was produced at Caerau, good quality steam coals were produced at Coegnant, Garth, Oakwood, St John's and Maesteg Deep, high-quality coking coal was produced at Caerau No.3 Pit, Garth, Oakwood, Maesteg Deep, and St John's, and high-quality house coal was produced at Coegnant, Maesteg Deep, St John's and Garth.

The production of steam coal for export was the most important element in the local economy from the 1890s to the 1920s. In the middle years of the nineteenth century the De La Beche–Playfair Trials had demonstrated to the Admiralty that South Wales coal was the most efficient fuel for steam-powered warships. By 1885, with large numbers of steam vessels in the fleet, the Admiralty had decided that South Wales would be the main supplier of coal to the Royal Navy. Apart from the large market that the Admiralty provided, the decision proved a great marketing boost for Welsh coal. However, some years before that Admiralty decision to rely

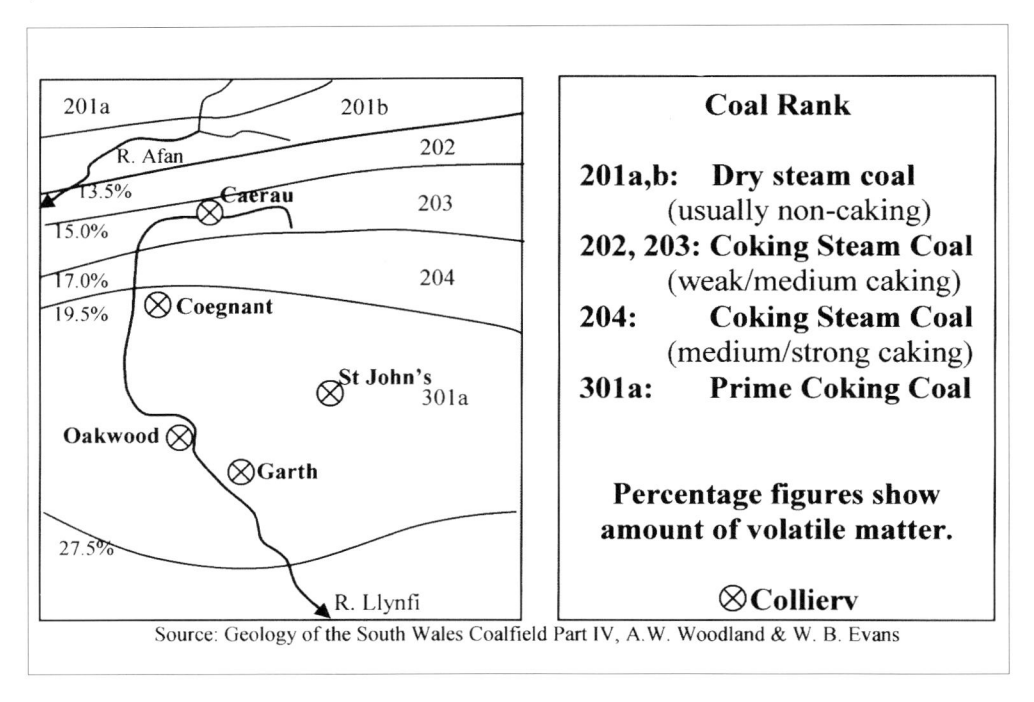

A classification of Llynfi Valley coals.

Coal Rank

- **201a,b:** Dry steam coal (usually non-caking)
- **202, 203:** Coking Steam Coal (weak/medium caking)
- **204:** Coking Steam Coal (medium/strong caking)
- **301a:** Prime Coking Coal

Percentage figures show amount of volatile matter.

Source: Geology of the South Wales Coalfield Part IV, A.W. Woodland & W. B. Evans

on Welsh steam coal, Llynfi Valley collieries were already contracted to supply the Royal Navy. In December 1868 for example, it was reported in the *Central Glamorgan Gazette* that George Moffatt, the chairman of the Llynvi Coal & Iron Co., 'had succeeded in getting the Llynvi Co. placed on the government list for the supply of coal to the Navy'.

The all-important Admiralty connection was formalised, after 1904, as the 'Admiralty List' of the twenty-six best steam coals. Although the 'List' appeared in all the trade journals of the time, it was not an official ranking of coal producers. When giving evidence to the Royal Commission on Coal Supplies in 1904, G.W. Miller, director of Naval Contracts, listed the coals purchased by the Admiralty. The trade press and the sales agencies immediately converted Miller's evidence into the 'Admiralty List' against which all steam coals were measured. The coal marketed as 'North's Imperial Navigation', produced at Caerau, was included on the prestigious listing and, as a result, the company could derive considerable benefit from being able to advertise its coals at home and abroad as a producer 'on the Admiralty List'.

The best steam coals left little ash after burning, and they were classed as 'smokeless' with a very high carbon content and very low percentages of volatile matter. The highest grade Caerau steam coal was ranked with those of the southern Rhondda district. During the First World War, although the number of coals on the published 'Admiralty List' did not change, about thirty additional high-quality steam coals were used by the Royal Navy due to the increased demand for fuel.

North's other higher grade steam coal, 'North's Navigation Smokeless', produced at Coegnant, St John's and Maesteg Deep, as well as a steam coal from Celtic Collieries were among the additional war-time Admiralty coals. Eventually, in 1922, the 'Celtic' brand produced at Garth was added to the published Admiralty List of the thirty-three best Welsh steam coals.

Analysis Figures for Llynfi Valley Steam Coals on the Admiralty List

Name of Coal	Fixed Carbon	Volatile Matter	Ash	Water	Sulphur
North's Imperial Navigation	79.52%	16.38%	3.09%	1.01%	0.95%
Celtic	70.67%	24.24%	4.12%	0.98%	0.98%

Source: 'S. Wales Coals', Llewellyn Davies and Owen Davies, Cardiff, 1924.

The contribution of North's Navigation Collieries to the steam coal trade was summarised in an article in *The South Wales Coal Annual* of 1917:

> The coals produced at the North's Collieries are principally steam descriptions of the best qualities, and possess a world-wide reputation. They are among those selected coals invariably contracted for by the British Admiralty authorities for consumption by the British Navy, but they are also in extensive demand for bunkering purposes by all the leading steamship companies of the world. Their calorific power is exceptionally high, and their chief markets are in the French, Mediterranean, and South American trades...

High-quality coke-making was also very important for both mining companies in the Llynfi Valley. Local coke was in great demand due to the natural qualities of the coal from the Maesteg district in particular, and the considerable investment made by the companies in coal preparation before coking took place at Maesteg Deep, Garth and Tondu. By the 1920s the valley was one of the largest centres of colliery-based coke production in the country. The merits of the coke produced in the Llynfi Valley were outlined when the National Coal Board made an assessment of North's Navigation Collieries at the time of nationalisation:

> The ovens produce an excellent foundry coke particularly suitable for high grade castings, which enjoys a wide reputation and commands the best price in the market. It is celebrated for its great purity and is the first choice of the foundry people in the Midlands. There is a complete absence of competition – since no coke of equal quality is produced elsewhere.

> **Annual Output about 1,250,000 Tons.**
>
> # NORTH'S NAVIGATION COLLIERIES
>
> (1889) LIMITED.
>
> **Exchange Buildings, CARDIFF.**
> (Sales Agents, LYSBERG LIMITED, CARDIFF.)
>
> SOLE PROPRIETORS AND SHIPPERS OF
>
> **NORTH'S IMPERIAL NAVIGATION**
> AND
> **NORTH'S NAVIGATION SMOKELESS STEAM COAL.**
>
> On the British Admiralty List for Home and Foreign Supplies.
>
> **NORTH'S FOUNDRY COKE**
> is used by the principal Engineering Firms and Government Arsenals, Dockyards, and Munition Works.
>
> **NORTH'S SMALL COALS**
> are of the Highest Quality and are used exclusively for Bunkers on many of the largest cargo carrying steamers
>
> SHIPPING PORTS:
> **PORT TALBOT, BARRY, CARDIFF & SWANSEA.**
> SHIPPING AGENTS.
> **LYSBERG LTD., PORT TALBOT & SWANSEA.**
>
> *Telegrams:—*
> "NORTH'S" Cardiff, Port Talbot. "PLISSON" Swansea.
> *Telephones:—*
> Cardiff, 5870 (Two lines.) Port Talbot, 128. Swansea, 873, Central.

An advertisement for North's Navigation Collieries from 1923.

The Maesteg area was also a major producer of house coal. A relatively small section of the *Two Feet Nine* seam worked at Maesteg Deep and Garth yielded what was regarded as the best house coal in South Wales. In 1924 William Phillips, a leading Cardiff coal buyer, wrote about the house coal from the Maesteg district: 'The *Two Feet Nine* seam yields ideal open grate and kitchen-range coal of tremendous power which is highly valued for its freedom from ash and its freedom from excessive smoke and soot'. Phillips regretted the fact that the 'ideal' properties of the coal were restricted to such a small section of the coalfield.

Thus the Llynfi Valley played an important role in the South Wales coal trade. However, although the pits served a range of markets, by 1924 there was a heavy bias towards the steam coal trade and the export market. By 1931 that over-emphasis on steam coal production would result in massive job losses, unemployment and short-time working.

CHAPTER ELEVEN

THE DECLINE OF COAL (1924–1939)

In 1924 7,080 men were employed in the six collieries of the upper Llynfi Valley. Of that total, 4,321 (61 per cent) were employed at the Caerau and Coegnant collieries producing mainly steam coal for the export trade. The three older, smaller mines at Maesteg Deep, Oakwood and Garth employed 1,305 (18 per cent). St John's, a modern colliery which served a wide range of markets, employed 1,473 (21 per cent). The local economy was thus vulnerably placed, with most miners dependent on the export trade, and with well over 1,000 men employed in three sixty-year-old mines which were approaching the end of their working lives.

Coal exports from South Wales had peaked in 1913 and there had been a brief period of relative prosperity in the coalfield after the First World War. During that post-war boom, in 1920, mining employment in the Llynfi Valley reached its peak of 7,327 miners. By 1921 there was a sharp drop in exports of coal. During 1923–4 a temporary surge in exports from South Wales occurred due to a prolonged miners' strike in the USA, and the French occupation of the Ruhr. The two events prevented the United States and Germany supplying the world market for coal, and South Wales benefited for a short time as a result.

After the brief revival of 1923–4, the South Wales coal export trade went into a marked decline. Because of the bias towards exports in the Llynfi Valley steam coal pits, the district was one of the most seriously affected areas in South Wales. The scale of the decline in mining employment can be seen from the graph on page 82. The pronounced decline from 1924–1930 was followed by the collapse of mining employment when the workforce was halved during 1930–1 with the loss of 2,500 jobs. Overall, between 1924 and 1931 the number of miners at work declined from 7,080 to 2,372 (66 per cent). With the decline of the coal trade, the fortunes of North's Navigation Collieries changed dramatically. Ambitious plans to develop new collieries around the old Park Slip site near Aberkenfig were shelved and profits fell sharply after 1923. The company operated at a loss from 1924 to 1928, and profits did not recover until 1933.

Graph showing the decline of employment in coal mining in the Llynfi Valley, 1924–31.
Source: Mines Dept: List of Mines, HMSO, 1925, 1928, 1931, 1932.

The reasons for the disastrous fall in employment were complex. Foreign competition in the form of Polish and German coal, for example, resulted in losses of markets abroad. Exports to the important Italian market fell sharply after 1918 as Italy imported German coal supplied as 'reparations' after the First World War. During the 1920s there was also less demand for Welsh coal in Italy due to increased production of hydro-electricity and the electrification of the railways. From North's ledgers for the years 1915–16, the Italian market was one of the company's most important. It is probable that the decline of that market contributed to large-scale job losses in the Llynfi Valley. The French market, probably the most important before the war, was increasingly supplied by German coal in the 1920s. In July 1931 the French government introduced restrictions on imports of coal, a move that seriously affected the South Wales coal trade.

Another factor was the uncompetitive price of South Wales coal. Because of difficult geological conditions, mining costs were high and, after 1925, when Britain returned to the gold standard, coal prices were even less competitive as sterling increased its value 10 per cent in foreign markets. Thus it was difficult for South Wales colliery companies to compete in markets abroad.

To add to the difficulties, the use of oil by shipping had been increasing after the war and, by the mid-1920s, the consumption of cheaper, more practical oil was greater than coal. The general decline of coal in the 1920s was accelerated after the Wall Street Crash of 1929 and the trade depression that followed.

During 1928 the recession in the coal industry, which began four years earlier, developed into the full-scale trade depression that would blight the Llynfi Valley and other coalfield communities for the next decade. As economic conditions deteriorated, the incidence of distress and poverty, which was previously associated with strike action or lock-outs, became part of the daily routine. As well as the usual items regarding sport, chapel activities and local gossip in the *Glamorgan Gazette,* harrowing references to the plight of many children in the Llynfi Valley were appearing all too frequently. In March 1928 for example, some time before the massive decline in local mining employment, a correspondent commented: '…already much distress is prevalent, and pale, weakly children underclothed, and some without boots on their feet, are sad sights that can be witnessed every day'.

During the early summer of 1928, in response to deteriorating market conditions and also in an attempt to reform the pay structure for North's workers, all the collieries in the Llynfi Valley with the exception of Garth ceased production. Caerau was closed on 14 May, and coal production was suspended at Coegnant and St John's on 28 June. According to North's Navigation, traditionally high wage rates in the Llynfi Valley prevented the company challenging their competitors in the shrinking market for coal. Before the Mines (Minimum Wage) Act of 1912, North's Navigation was already paying a minimum wage that was higher than the rate set by the Act. After 1912 the differential was maintained so, according to the company, Llynfi Valley miners were among the highest paid in the coalfield. Early in September, as a result of a meeting between D.R. Llewellyn of North's, and the miners' representative Vernon Hartshorn MP, the colliers accepted a 6½ per cent drop in wages and North's collieries re-opened. The reduction lowered wage rates in the valley to the national minimum level. After the agreement Oakwood did not re-open. Faced with depletion of resources, high mining costs and competitive markets, Oakwood Colliery, which had first produced coal in 1869, was the first of the three older mines in the valley to fall victim to the trade depression.

Coal production ceased at Maesteg Deep in 1930 and, in March 1930, Celtic Collieries Ltd, the owners of Garth, went into receivership. A successful future for Garth had been predicted during the early 1920s when Celtic Collieries leased the sizeable 'Moel Gilau Taking' from the Dunraven Estate. This new extension to the Garth mineral estate covered a large area to the east of Llety Brongu and to the north of the Port Talbot Railway. The colliery company intended to develop the extensive reserves of coal in the *No. 3 Rhondda* seam in this new district. Developments at Garth were evidently not a great success as, on 16 Monday September 1930, the colliery was closed as the receiver could not find a buyer for the mine, having turned down an offer from Cory Brothers. From reports in the *Glamorgan Advertiser*, the day shift had worked normally on that Monday but when the night shift arrived at the mine, the closure was announced and the men 'were turned back'. Although the colliery had been in receivership for six months and the men were on day-to-day contracts, the decision still came as a shock for the workforce and the community in Garth. There had been no hint of closure from the receiver until the sudden announcement to the night shift. After over sixty years in production the demise of Garth Colliery was swift. On the day after the closure announcement, the men were told to remove their tools from the mine and the horses were taken to other collieries in the district. A few weeks later, in November, the workings were abandoned and, in the same month, Messrs Cohen of Neath were awarded the contract to clear the site. At the time of the closures, 639 jobs were lost at Garth and over 100 at Maesteg Deep, although a very small workforce was retained there as the drift mine was kept open for pumping.

Caerau Colliery, which had specialised in the production of high grade Admiralty steam coal, suffered most in the 'Locust Years' of the late 1920s and early 1930s. After the closure of the smaller No.3 Pit in 1925, the colliery still employed over 1,800 in 1927. By 1930 the number had dropped to 1,585, and had collapsed to 469 a year later. The colliery worked intermittently during 1931 and coal production was suspended in January 1932. Just forty-two men were employed on maintenance work there in 1933; the pit was re-opened in January 1934. From figures in the government's annual List of Mines it appears that when coal production was suspended at Caerau the remaining workforce could have transferred to Coegnant.

Employment totals levelled off during 1931–3 and increased slightly in 1934 with the resumption of coal production at Caerau. During the years of decline St John's Colliery suffered least; the mine was less dependent on the export trade and served a broader range of markets. By 1934 the numbers of miners at St John's had only dropped 8 per cent from the peak employment figures at the colliery in the early 1920s. There was a relatively small scale improvement in employment totals by 1936 as there were 650 more miners at work than during the dark days of 1931–3. Caerau Colliery, with only forty-two workers listed for 1933, employed 455 in 1936.

During the difficult years of the 1930s the steam coal districts of South Wales were among the most seriously affected in Britain. By 1929 the unemployment rate in the Llynfi Valley had risen to 28 per cent and, during the early 1930s, the district experienced levels of unemployment in excess of 40 per cent. Even in 1938, after some improvement in the economic situation, 20 per cent were unemployed in the Maesteg district, and in Caerau the figure was 41 per cent. Because of the high levels of unemployment during the late 1920s and for most of the 1930s, poverty and uncertainty had replaced the relative stability of the years before 1924.

THE DECLINE OF EMPLOYMENT AT THE COLLIERIES 1924–1931

Colliery	Workforce 1924	Workforce 1931	Job Losses 1924–31
Caerau	2,388	469	1,919 (-80%)
Coegnant	1,914	691	1,223 (-64%)
St. John's	1,473	1,223	250 (-17%)
Maesteg Deep	277	Closed 1930	277
Garth	753	Closed 1930	753
Oakwood	275	Closed 1928	275
Total	7,080	2,383	4,697 (-66%)

Source: Mines Dept: List of Mines, HMSO, 1925 and 1932.

The unemployed men who remained in the district faced years without work, especially in the period 1928–34. Others left the area to seek employment in the new light industries growing up, for example, in the Midlands and west London. Between the census years of 1921 and 1931 the population of the Maesteg Urban District dropped by 3,347 or 12 per cent.

Even for those in employment, short-time working was commonplace in the 1930s. From time to time it was noted in company ledgers that days were lost due to 'Trade Depression'. In June 1936, for example, ten days were lost at Caerau, six at Coegnant and four at St John's. As late as June 1938 Coegnant and Caerau lost ten days each, and four were lost at St John's.

As unemployment levels increased in the late 1920s, local and national initiatives attempted to alleviate the growing problem of acute poverty. In August 1928, for example, the Maesteg sub-committee of the Mining Areas Relief Fund was set up, and, in October 1930, major local road-building schemes were approved which provided work for the unemployed. In March 1932, the first of a number of local road projects was completed when the mile-long 'bypass' was opened from Picton Street in Nantyffyllon to a junction with Neath Road near the General Hospital.

Although the efforts of voluntary organisations and the various public works schemes were positive attempts to ease the problem of widespread unemployment, the existing infrastructure set in place to manage the problem of poverty was overwhelmed by the economic crisis. Looking back from the early twenty-first century, after sixty years of the Welfare State in Britain, it is difficult to fully appreciate the alarming plight of the pre-war unemployed and their families. In the late 1920s long-term unemployment could lead to destitution as, after twenty-six weeks, state benefits were withdrawn so miners and their families had no option but to seek assistance from the local board of guardians, a relic of earlier Poor Law legislation.

As the government attempted to cope with the problem of unemployment and the expense of unemployment relief, new legislation was introduced in the early 1930s. The boards of guardians were disbanded and the workhouses they administered passed into the control of the local authority. In 1934 unemployment benefit became available to the long-term unemployed through a rigorous system of means testing which simply added to the difficulties of the time.

A report in the *Glamorgan Advertiser* in February 1930 gives some indication of the plight of the long-term unemployed in the early years of the Depression. On Saturday 1 February, four unemployed Caerau miners, representing the Maesteg Area Council of the National Unemployed Workers Movement (NUWM), were 'received' by the Bridgend and Cowbridge board of guardians. The men were concerned that the long-term unemployed lost their benefit after six months and were forced to subsist on the relief provided by the board, which was below the inadequate level of unemployment benefit. The attention of the board was also drawn to the plight of single unemployed men over forty. After their six month's benefit ended, the board's relieving officers were only able to offer the men a place at the Bridgend Workhouse. The deputation also informed the board that families in receipt of relief could not afford to buy coal, and requested that the guardians supply fuel to families in need.

From the report, we can see that the Dickensian board of guardians and the local workhouse were very much part of the outmoded system of support for the unemployed in the late 1920s and early 1930s. At the end of January 1930 for example, in addition to those claiming unemployment benefit, 3,776 people were dependent on the board of guardians in the Bridgend district, and there were 272 people in the Bridgend Workhouse. The crisis did give rise to change as the boards of guardians had disappeared by 1931, but it would be another fourteen years before the Beveridge Report heralded a new era and a Welfare State.

The local branch of the NUWM was also actively engaged in the organisation of the many hunger marches that took place during the 1930s. A Caerau contingent, for example, was among the hundred or so campaigners on the South Wales Hunger March to the TUC Conference at Bristol in September 1931. The march was broken up by mounted police near the conference hall and the TUC refused to meet a deputation of six of the marchers.

One of the most demoralising results of long-term unemployment in the valley during the bleakest years of the Depression was the high incidence of enforced eviction from rented accommodation. Uncompromising landlords wasted no time in removing the unemployed and their families from rented premises, often placing their furniture and other possessions on the roadside. The problem was particularly acute in the Caerau district where unemployment levels were among the highest in Britain during the years 1932–4. The evictions prompted protest meetings at Caerau Library and in the adjacent Library Road during January and February 1932. Some of the meetings were organised by Llwydarth-born Idris Cox, a prominent figure in the Communist Party of Great Britain, who became editor of the *Daily Worker* in the mid-1930s. The protests, and the activities of the Communist organisers, were closely monitored by the police officer in charge of the Maesteg sub-division, Inspector Parry, who painstakingly ensured that public order was maintained whatever the local circumstances.

The role of the police at public meetings in the Caerau district became a significant issue in the mid-1930s and resulted in well-publicised appeal proceedings at the High Court. A well-attended meeting organised by the International Labour Defence Organisation at Caerau Library on 17 August 1934 ended in disarray when the presence of three police officers at the meeting was challenged by the organisers. A formal request had been made that the police should not attend the meeting and, after scuffles in the hall and the arrival of a further fourteen police officers from Caerau Police Station, allegations of assault were made by the police against one of the organisers and vice versa. The case came before the Bridgend magistrates and during the proceedings the police contended that they had a right to enter and remain in the hall as, from previous experience of political meetings in Caerau, 'there was a risk of unlawful assembly, breaches of the peace could occur, and seditious and inflammatory speeches were likely to be made'. The local magistrates supported the police action, and the claim by one of the organisers that he had been assaulted by the police at the meeting was dismissed. However in May 1935 an appeal against the magistrates' verdict was heard at the High Court. The appeal proceedings attracted the attention of the national press as the case challenged the right of the police to enter public meetings on private premises. Such was the importance of the case that the Caerau appellant was represented by Sir Stafford Cripps KC and Dingle Foot KC, and the appeal was heard before the Lord Chief Justice together with Mr Justice Avory and Mr Justice Lawrence. As all three agreed with the magistrates' opinion, the case was again dismissed.

In addition to poverty and uncertainty, rhetoric and litigation, the trade depression brought tragedy to the Llynfi Valley when three unemployed miners were killed while attempting to cut much-needed coal on a hillside outcrop in September 1931. The three men, two from Caerau and one from Abercregan, were in a group of twenty-one unemployed miners working the coal outcrops near the head of the valley from old levels. The three entered the workings at midnight with the intention of cutting coal through the night. Shortly after they reached the coal face the workings collapsed, burying all three. Despite the efforts of the miners in the adjacent levels and a rescue team from Caerau Colliery, two men were suffocated by the fall and the third died of his injuries some hours later.

CHAPTER TWELVE

THE END OF COAL MINING

The mining workforce in the Llynfi Valley remained at about 2,600 until the end of the Second World War. After the war, the nationalised coal industry in the valley was gradually transformed as mechanisation replaced the 'traditional' labour intensive methods of cutting coal. Up to the 1920s coal was hand-cut, or had been brought down by explosives, and was then 'hand-filled' into trams that were hauled to the bottom of the shaft for winding. During the 1920s, underground conveyors began to replace the traditional journeys of trams underground, but progress was slow and it was not until the 1950s that coal production was revolutionised by new technologies. During that decade traditional methods of cutting and filling coal began to be replaced, on quite a large scale, by mechanised, self-advancing cutting and 'power loading' systems. Mechanised mining involved setting hydraulic props to support the roof before operating the cutting machines at the coal face. At the face, hydraulic rams pushed forward the cutting machine and its flexible armoured conveyors. The conveyors received and carried away the coal that fell as the cutting machine passed along the coal face. By the mid-1950s mechanisation was developing rapidly, and the first power loading agreement between the Coal Board and the South Wales NUM was drawn up in September 1956. During that year 12 per cent of British coal production was power loaded; by 1966 the figure was 84 per cent. The transformation of coal production during the late 1950s and the 1960s was marked by the signing of the 'National Power Loading Agreement' by the NUM and the NCB in June 1967.

After the war the local coal industry also enjoyed a period of relative prosperity. The Llynfi Valley was unique in the South Wales Coalfield as there were no pit closures in the district during a forty-seven year period from 1930 to 1977, a time when scores of mines were abandoned across the coalfield. The area was fortunate in that domestic markets for power station steam coal and for high-quality coking coal expanded in the post-war period. Also the *Gelli Deg* seam, the lowest major seam in the coal measures, had not been worked extensively in the Llynfi Valley; it was fully developed by the National Coal Board after 1951. Before the development of the new seam the future of St John's Colliery had been in doubt. The *Gelli Deg* seam yielded high-quality coking coal which was in great demand at integrated steel plants at Port Talbot and

The end of mining in the Llynfi Valley. The South Pit head frame tower at St John's Colliery in January 1986 prior to demolition, with the wall plaque set in place to mark the sinking of the shaft seventy-seven years before.

Llanwern. At St John's the seam had a sound roof and was worked from mechanised faces during the 1960s and 1970s at relatively low cost. Such was the importance of the *Gelli Deg* at St John's that, in 1963, for example, 88 per cent of the colliery output was derived from that seam. During the 1960s the National Coal Board closed seventy-four collieries in South Wales and concentrated investment at a small number of 'long life' pits. Coegnant and St John's, in particular, benefited from that strategy.

Although the workforce was much smaller than in the 1920s, in many ways the 1950s and 1960s were the most successful years for the Llynfi Valley miners. It was a time of full employment, and the hopes of generations of mineworkers had been realised in the post-war period when the collieries were nationalised. Also health care was freely available to all, there was greater educational opportunity, better quality housing and generally improved living standards. In addition, at long last, pit-head baths were provided for all the Llynfi Valley colliers during the mid-1950s.

In 1962, 2,336 men were employed in the three local collieries, a similar figure to the total thirty years before. Just over 2,000 were employed in 1976, and over the next nine years those jobs would be lost as coal mining came to an end in the Llynfi Valley. Caerau closed in 1977, Coegnant in 1981 and St John's in 1985. The reasons for the relatively quick demise of mining in less than a decade after a 150 year span of productivity were complex. Geological difficulties at Coegnant and the exhaustion of the *Gelli Deg* seam at St John's were important factors. Foreign, often subsidised, competition in the coking coal market was another. Also the availability of American and Australian coking coal, cheaply produced from open-cast sites and shipped at low cost to South Wales in bulk carriers, was significant. In addition, electricity production required less coal as more gas-fired power stations came on-stream. Perhaps of equal importance was the withdrawal of government support for coal mining as socio-economic considerations were replaced by privatisation and the market-driven strategies that emerged in the mid-1980s.

Caerau

Blaenllynfi
(c.1855-72)

Caerau
(1890-1977)

Tygwyn-bach
(c.1846-1906)

Coegnant
(1881-1981)

Tywith
(1846-84)

Maesteg Deep
(1868-1930)

Caedefaid
(1867-1908)

St John's
(1908-1985)

Nantyffyllon

Dyffryn Madoc
(c1850-1878)

Gin Pit
(c.1850-1875)

Maesteg Ironworks
No.1 Pit
(c.1850-60)

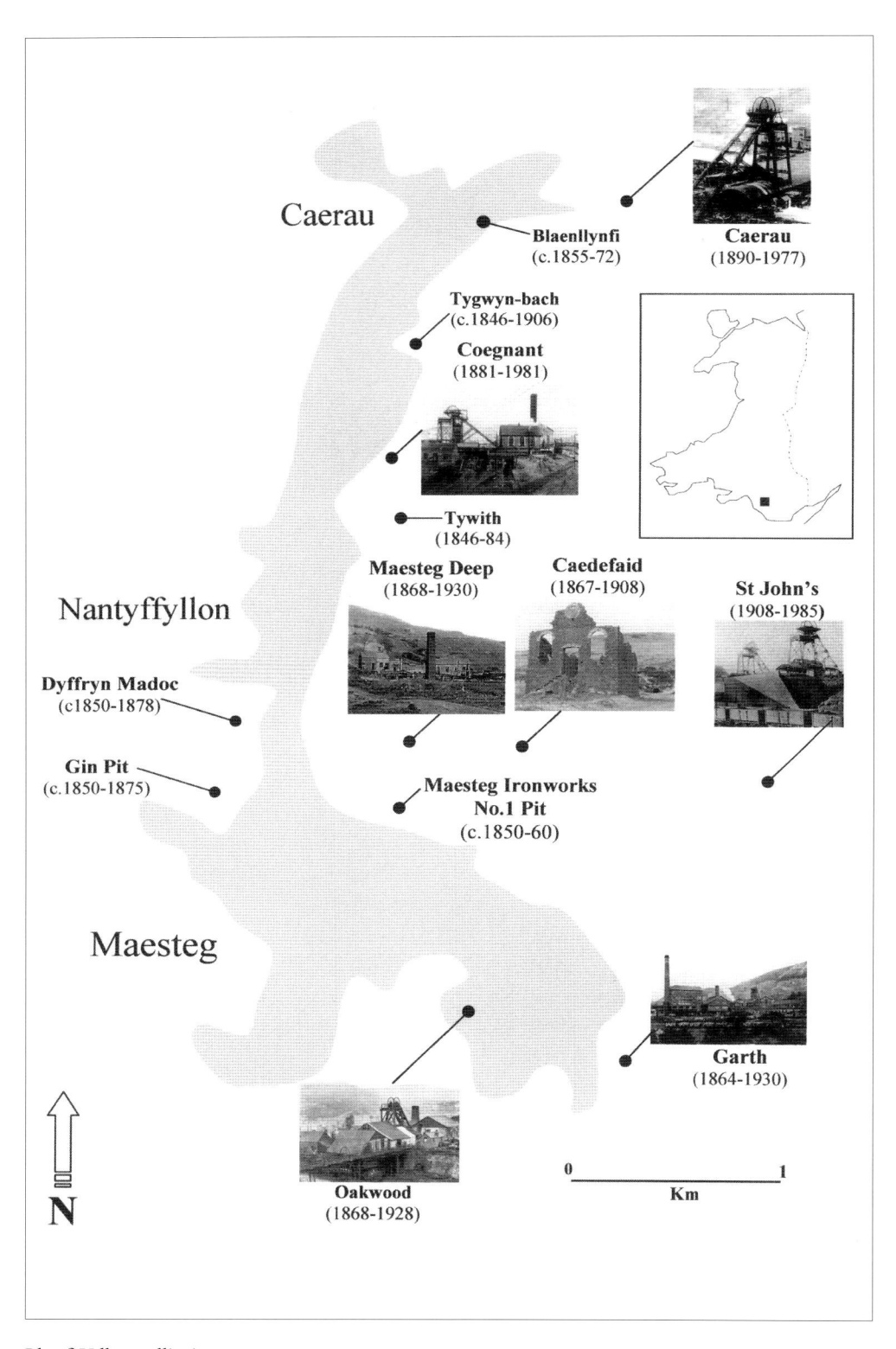

Maesteg

Garth
(1864-1930)

0　　　　　　　1
Km

N

Oakwood
(1868-1928)

Llynfi Valley collieries, 1846–1985

PART TWO

THE COLLIERIES

CAEDEFAID COLLIERY 1867–1908
NGR SS863918

The early history of the Caedefaid Colliery is difficult to be precise about. It was probably opened up as a small level in the 1840s or 1850s. In December 1859 a fatal accident at the Caedefaid Level, Maesteg Ironworks, was reported in the *Bridgend Chronicle*. That mine was located near the outcrop of the *Caedefaid* seam on the hillside above the works. The 'more modern' Caedefaid Colliery, or No.9 Level, was possibly the redevelopment of those workings by the Llynvi Coal & Iron Co. in 1867. The level had been driven 1,860 yards into the hillside during 1866–7 and was formally opened in October 1867. The mine was numbered in the sequence used by the Llynvi Coal & Iron Co. Ltd. Coal was produced from the *Caedefaid* and *Victoria* seams and black-band iron ore production was also very important during the period 1867 to 1884.

The tunnel in the photograph below was the intake airway. The return airway was a parallel tunnel with an offset ventilation drift to the surface. Fresh air was drawn through the workings by the draught from a furnace-fire near the mouth of the ventilation drift. However, shortly after opening, in 1868, a Waddle Fan was installed. The fan was probably the first to operate in the valley. The colliery changed hands three times during the years 1872 to 1880 and was bought by North's Navigation in 1889. It was the most important colliery in the Llynfi Valley during the 1880s with a workforce of about 400. As deep mining developed in the 1890s and North's worked the lower seams in the valley, the No.9 Level gradually became less important and eventually closed in 1908.

The engine house of the No.9 Level in the 1960s with the entrance adit (bottom right) which gave access to the Caedefaid seam. Three other major seams outcropped on the hillside above the mine.

CAERAU COLLIERY 1890–1977
NGR SS866945

Caerau Colliery was the first major development undertaken by North's Navigation Collieries (1889) Ltd. The new company was keen to develop the reserves of high grade steam coal at the head of the Llynfi Valley, and sinking commenced in 1890. The North and South Pits were initially sunk to the *Six Feet* seam at 340 yards. The South Pit was the upcast ventilating shaft.

The initial development of the colliery was hampered by an industrial dispute over coal-cutting rates that lasted from April 1894 to February 1896. After the strike eventually ended, the progress of the colliery was spectacular and, in 1904, coal from the Caerau Pits was included on the prestigious 'Admiralty List' of the twenty-six best steam coals. The coal was marketed with the brand name 'North's Imperial Navigation'.

As the colliery developed, the new mining township of Caerau expanded rapidly during the period 1895–1910. During 1906–7 a third shaft, the No.3 Pit, was sunk to the general-purpose *Caedefaid* seam at 167 yards.

In the early 1920s the two steam coal pits were deepened to the *Lower New (Bute)* seam, and the colliery's employment peak of 2,432 mine-workers was reached in 1922. Of that total, 329 were employed at the No.3 Pit, about 13 per cent of the Caerau Colliery workforce. During the late 1920s and early 1930s, as coal exports declined, the fortunes of the Caerau Pits changed dramatically. The No.3 Pit closed in 1925, and coal production was suspended at the colliery during 1932–34. The mine re-opened in the latter year with a much smaller workforce and the colliery remained in production with an average labour force of about 560 men until closure in 1977.

Caerau Colliery, 1952, from right to left: South Pit, North Pit, No.3 Pit.

The Development of the Colliery

In the photograph below from around 1906, sixteen years after sinking had commenced on the site, the colliery is still in the early stages of development. The South Pit to the right of the photograph has been completed but the North Pit to the left is unfinished. There are no large sheaves (or pulley wheels) at the top of North Pit head frame and the engine that was used to sink the North Pit in the early 1890s remains in place. The winding gear originally used by the sinkers, with small sheaves, is still inside the head frame tower. Plans to develop the North Pit were evidently suspended although North's Navigation intended to eventually complete the pit by deepening the shaft. The small structure at 'X' is the sinkers' rig for the No.3 Pit which was sunk during 1906–7.

In the view below (1912) the No.3 Pit, with its head frame to the left, has been completed. Around ten years later the North Pit was deepened and finally completed with 20ft-diameter sheaves in the 70ft-head frame tower.

Caerau Colliery, around 1906.

Caerau Colliery, around 1912.

CAERAU COLLIERY

Caerau Colliery: the first forty years. A view from c.1900 with the colliery in the early stage of development.

Caerau Colliery: the first forty years. A view from a similar position in 1930 with the South Pit to the left. The No.3 Pit, which was completed in February 1908, occupies the foreground and the large conical tip, known locally as the 'Amy Johnson', forms a backdrop to the South Pit head frame tower. The North Pit headgear has been completed and a power station has been added to the site with a cooling tower at 'X'. In 1920 the station was capable of generating 1.5MW of electricity and, during the 1920s and 1930s, the colliery supplied electricity to Maesteg Urban District Council for domestic use locally. In the early 1920s Caerau Colliery was one of the largest in South Wales with about 2,400 workers.

The Caerau pit-head baths under construction in 1952. The colliery had already been in production for sixty years when the building was formally opened in March 1954.

A view of the surface at Caerau Colliery in 1957. The engine house at 'Y' is being enlarged to accommodate electric winders, the fan-house is at 'X' and the colliery workshops at 'Z'.

Repair work on the extensive colliery sidings in 1950, with the Caerau township in the background.

A view of 'Croker's Double' (Parting) at Caerau Colliery in the early 1950s. A double parting was a section of railway underground where journeys of trams could pass each other. To the left empty trams are waiting to be hauled to the coal face, and to the right full trams are en route to the cage at the pit-bottom.

COEGNANT COLLIERY 1881–1981
NGR SS856934

Coegnant Colliery had the longest working life of all the Llynfi Valley mines. Of the three large deep mines in the valley, it was the only one with links to the Maesteg iron industry. After the voluntary liquidation of the Llynvi, Tondu & Ogmore Coal & Iron Co. in 1878, the receiver, J.J. Smith, re-formed the venture as the Llynvi & Tondu Co. in 1880. The new company began sinking the Coegnant pits in 1881 on the site of two shafts that had been unsuccessfully developed, probably in the 1850s. By June 1883 the North Pit had been successfully sunk to the *Caerau (Seven Feet)* seam at 150 yards.

In 1889, after the demise of the Llynvi & Tondu Co. and the closure of the Llynfi Ironworks, the ownership of the mine passed to North's Navigation Collieries Ltd. At the time of the take-over, the colliery employed about 400 workers.

During 1903–4 the mine was modernised; the shafts were widened and the South Pit was deepened to the *Lower New (Bute)* seam at 244 yards. The redeveloped colliery is shown in the photograph on page 99; the North Pit on the left was the upcast ventilating shaft. The mine prospered during the period 1900 to 1924 with a peak workforce of 2,182 in 1914. After the collapse of the steam coal trade in the late 1920s and early 1930s, the pits remained in production with a much reduced average workforce of 825 during the late 1930s.

When the National Coal Board took over the colliery in 1947 the North Pit was listed as 178 yards deep (151 yards to the winding level), and the South Pit was 374 yards deep (362). Evidently the South Pit had been further deepened, probably in the early 1920s.

After the Second World War the colliery produced mainly semi-coking coal which was blended into coking mixtures for the steel industry. In the mid-1950s the mine was modernised and the North Pit was deepened. In the 1970s, almost a century after the colliery was opened, some seams faced exhaustion and the workings were plagued by geological problems as new, less accessible districts were opened up.

In the search for new resources, mining operations crossed the Pen-y-Castell fault as the coal reserves to the west of the river Llynfi were developed. The seams to the east of the river, which had been worked since the 1880s, were displaced downwards more than 150 yards on the west side of the valley due to the fault.

Towards the end of its working life the colliery was dependent on the semi-coking coal of the *Lower Nine Feet (Upper New)* seam. The annual output of coal was 100,000 tonnes with a workforce of about 500. Geological difficulties, particularly faulting, eventually led to the closure of the colliery in 1981.

Coegnant Colliery, around 1908. *Inset:* One of North's distinctive red-painted monogram coal wagons of the period 1895–1910.

The first pit-head baths in the Llynfi Valley at Coegnant in 1939, the year the building was opened. As well as the baths, the building housed a canteen, and a medical centre was added a few years later. After almost sixty years of hardship for generations of workers at the colliery, the new range of amenities transformed the daily routine of Coegnant colliers and their families.

General view of the Spelter district in 1897, before the redevelopment of the colliery. The original fan house, with a 40ft Guibal fan, is shown to the right of the colliery chimney.

A view from a similar location, c.1940, with the pit-head baths to the left and housing and allotment gardens occupying the former pasture land along the valley floor.

Coegnant Colliery in June 1956. A view of the South Pit shortly before the winding engine house on the right, with its steam-powered winder, was enlarged to accommodate electric winding equipment.

Coegnant North Pit June 1956, with cladding in the head frame tower. As the pit was the upcast ventilation shaft the cladding formed part of the airtight seal at the top of the shaft that ensured the efficiency of the ventilation system.

The south side of Coegnant Colliery in the mid-1950s with the cooling tower for the original colliery power station in the background. Until the development of the National Grid, the surplus electricity generated at Coegnant, like its Caerau neighbour, was supplied to the local Urban District Council.

The power-house at Coegnant in 1981. The building was constructed in 1912 to house the generators and compressors that supplied electricity and compressed air to the haulage systems underground. It was thus an early example of the application of new sources of energy in the coal industry. By 1920, for instance, one 500hp electric-powered haulage engine was located near the bottom of the North Pit and two 300hp electric-powered engines hauled coal to the bottom of the South Pit. The 'inner haulages' were worked by compressed air.

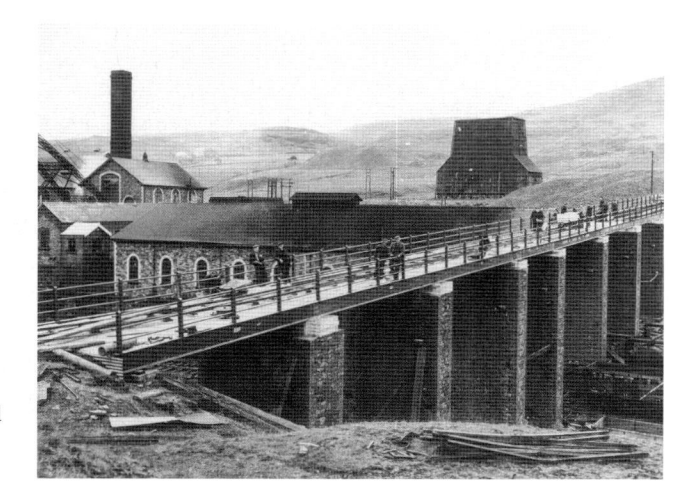

Two views of the dram circuit at Coegnant, May 1953.

Above: Creeper mechanisms (the top of one system is shown on the left), and carefully graded slopes, such as the gradual incline to the right, allowed drams to circulate efficiently around the top of the pit.

Below: Another view of the split-level arrangement that allowed the movement of coal after it reached the top of the shaft. After weighing, loaded drams moved by gravity into slow-turning tipplers like the one to the right, which emptied the coal into railway wagons below, or onto screens for grading in the era before the development of central coal preparation plants. The empty dram then moved on, by gravity, to the base of a creeper mechanism, such as the one to the left, which raised it to an upper level. It then rolled down the gradient to be used again.

Installing a new winder drum at Coegnant North Pit in July 1957.

View of part of the surface at Coegnant in June 1956, with pit wood stocks and the colliery saw-mills (top right). In 1950 there were 128 men employed on the surface, about 19 per cent of the workforce.

Two views of Coegnant Colliery at the time of closure in 1981.

Right: View from the north-west with the unusual concrete-clad South Pit head frame tower to the right.

Below: View from the south-east. The hundred-year-old colliery and its immediate surroundings formed the oldest continuously developed industrial site in the Llynfi Valley with coal levels and the site of a nearby spelter works dating back to 1830.

GARTH COLLIERY 1864–1930
NGR SS868902

Garth was sunk in about 1864 by John Brogden & Sons primarily to supply coking coal to their ironworks at Tondu. The Brogden properties were sold to the Llynvi, Tondu & Ogmore Coal & Iron Co. in 1872, and, with the demise of that company in 1878, Garth was probably closed during the trade depression of the late 1870s and early 1880s.

By 1883 the mine had been re-opened by a new owner, James Humby, trading as Garth Merthyr Steam Navigation Collieries Ltd. The company seems to have been re-formed in 1887 when the mine was owned by a partnership that included James Barrow, Richard and John Cory of Cardiff and Ebenezer Lewis of Newport.

The colliery was worked with limited success until it was bought in 1900 by Sir Alfred Jones of the Elder Dempster shipping company. Sir Alfred purchased Garth and Oakwood to supply his large fleet of steamers with bunker coals, and the new venture traded as Elder's Navigation Collieries Ltd. Elder's deepened the colliery to the *Bute* seam at 373 yards, redeveloped the surface, installed sixty Coppee coke ovens and built a large, modern coal washery on the site. After the death of Sir Alfred Jones in 1909, Elder's retained the ownership of Garth, although the company name was changed to Celtic Collieries Ltd in 1915. A year later Celtic Collieries Ltd was bought by Lord Rhondda's Cambrian Combine.

Garth Colliery, 1907, with the South Pit headgear to the right, and the washery in the centre of the photograph.

Garth Colliery, pictured around 1899, before the redevelopment of the surface by Elder's Navigation Collieries.

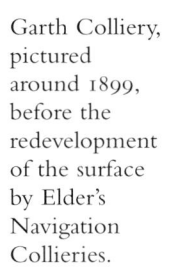

The years from 1916 to 1924 were the most successful in the history of the Garth pits, but, with the decline of the steam coal export trade in the late 1920s, Celtic Collieries went into receivership in March 1930 and Garth closed in September of that year.

The Development of the Garth Site
In the rare, early view of Garth Colliery shown above, the North Pit is on the left and both pits seem to have their winding houses in a central position between the two head frame towers. The North Pit (upcast) has a very basic wooden head frame, the South Pit tower is more substantial though probably timber-framed. There appears to be a Waddle ventilation fan to the left (marked 'X').

By 1906 Garth had been extensively re-modelled; the surface arrangements at the colliery were completely re-designed and both head frame towers were rebuilt. The South Pit tower was replaced with a wrought-iron structure. In about 1905 a new winding house was built in the background of this view, and the South Pit tower was turned through ninety degrees and re-aligned with the new winding engine. The future position of the new South Pit winding house is shown by a dotted line in the illustration above. As the site was redeveloped, coke ovens and a washery were constructed on the derelict land in the right foreground, probably during the years 1900–2.

For sixteen years (1900–1916), the Garth and Oakwood collieries were part of the Elder Dempster group of companies that was largely built-up by Sir Alfred Jones during the years 1890–1909. The group included subsidiaries producing and supplying bunker fuel as well as a number of well-known shipping lines such as Elders and Fyffes and the British and African Steam Navigation Co. Steam coal was produced at the group's Llynfi Valley collieries and bunker fuel was supplied along the west African routes to coaling stations that were managed by agencies owned by Alfred Jones. The three most important were the Grand Canary Coaling Co., the Tenerife Coaling Co. and the Sierra Leone Coaling Co. After the death of Sir Alfred Jones in 1909, Elder Dempster, and the two mines, became part of the Royal Mail group of companies under the leadership of Lord Kylsant. The Royal Mail group sold the collieries in 1916.

Loaded coal wagons on the Port Talbot Railway near Garth Colliery, around 1901.

The redevelopment of Garth Colliery, around 1904. The washery has been completed to the left of the main chimney, and the South Pit winding house is under construction. The South Pit head frame tower has yet to be re-aligned.

The completed pit-head, pictured around 1906, with a new head frame tower. The two photographs above, and the previous view of 1899, clearly illustrate the transformation of the surface from the rather primitive conditions shown in 1899 to the modern colliery of 1906.

GARTH COLLIERY

Self-acting tramway installed during the redevelopment of Garth by Elder's Navigation Collieries. The trams are 'marked-up' with colliers' numbers and weights of large coal.

The Garth coke ovens and washery in 1920. The headgear of the North Pit is shown in the centre of the photograph.

Advertisements for Garth Colliery and the Elder Dempster Shipping Line.

MAESTEG DEEP COLLIERY 1868–1930
NGR SS859919

The early history of Maesteg Deep Colliery is difficult to trace. The first colliery on the site was probably opened in about 1868 by the Llynvi Coal & Iron Co. It was known as 'Moffatt's Level' after George Moffatt MP, the chairman of the company, and by 1873 it was referred to as 'Moffatt's Slip'. The mine was first listed as 'Maesteg Deep' in 1875 although it was marked as 'Cwrt-y-Mwnws Colliery' on the first edition of the local large-scale Ordnance Survey map which was based on a survey of 1875–6. From the name changes it seems that the original level was deepened to a slip or slant in the early 1870s.

Maesteg Deep seems to have remained in production during the trade depression of the late 1870s and early 1880s as it was listed in the government's 'Mineral Statistics' during that period. It was owned by the Llynvi, Tondu & Ogmore Coal & Iron Co. from 1872 to 1878, and then by the Llynvi & Tondu Co. until it was taken over by North's Navigation in 1889. It appears that the mine was redeveloped and deepened by North's during 1890. In that year the colliery was out of production and colliery reports refer to 'drifting' taking place.

The drift, with a gradient of 1:6, intercepted the famous *Two Feet Nine* seam at 800 yards, and for forty years or so the colliery was associated with the celebrated house coal mined from that seam which was marketed as 'North's Best Maesteg Deep House coal'. The colliery was at its peak during the years 1907 to 1920 with a maximum workforce of 671 in 1910. Maesteg Deep closed in 1930.

The production of coke, especially high-quality foundry coke, was an important element in the local economy until the 1940s. North's coking coal was processed at Maesteg Deep and Tondu. Coal from the Maesteg district, particularly the small coal, was ideal for the coking process, which involved carbonising the coal in air-tight ovens. The controlled temperatures and the lack of oxygen in the ovens prevented the ignition of the coal yet allowed volatile matter (gas and tar) to be burned off or re-processed. The resulting coke, with 90–95 per cent carbon content and very small amounts of volatile material, was ideal for blast furnaces and foundries.

At Maesteg Deep there was a battery of 100 Coppee ovens, a Coppee Washery and a Sheppard's Washery. The coal was prepared at the washeries (on the right of the photograph on page 112), and loaded into hoppers. Trucks filled up at the hoppers and the ovens were top-loaded via a railway along the top of the battery. At the end of the coke-making process the rail-mounted ram on the right moved along the battery, pushing the carbonised coal out of each of the ovens in turn.

The two chimney stacks were demolished in around 1946 and the area was re-developed as a modern coal washery. The site was cleared in 1990 and reclaimed for housing and a new secondary school during 2003/4.

Maesteg Deep Colliery, pictured arouond 1916, with a journey of filled trams emerging from the drift mine. Cwrt-y-Mwnws farmhouse is shown behind the colliery buildings.

Airway (probably the main return airway) at Maesteg Deep Colliery in 1962 when the mine was still used for pumping. The pumping operation was abandoned in 1969 and the colliery site was cleared in 1972.

Part of a rare publicity photograph, probably taken in 1916, recovered from a well-worn printing plate, promoting the Park Coal Co. of Cardiff and Maesteg Deep house coal. The lorries are lined up in front of the Cardiff City Hall and the Maesteg Deep brand name is carried on the fronts of the vehicles.

The coke ovens and washery at Maesteg Deep Colliery, 1920.

The central washery, Maesteg, 1971. Up to the early years of the twentieth century most collieries had their own screens on site which allowed some grading of the coal before sale, and in later years many of the larger collieries developed their own preparation plants. As the three Llynfi Valley deep mines were quite close together and served similar markets, the National Coal Board centralised local coal preparation at the old Maesteg Deep site in 1957. The washery closed in 1988.

Coal could be easily moved between the collieries and the washery via the remaining sections of North's Internal Railway system and the old Port Talbot Railway. The train from St John's Colliery in this photograph of August 1983 is using the former Port Talbot Railway line to transfer coal to Maesteg washery. The Turberville housing estate is to the right.

Steam locomotives at work at Maesteg washery in the 1970s.

Above: Two of the six tank engines at work in the Llynfi Valley in 1971. Both were Hunslet 0-6-0STs and the locomotives were used for shunting and for hauling coal trains along the five miles of mineral railway that linked the collieries, the washery and the BR line.

Below: Tank engines in tandem as a large coal train is moved up the gradient to the washery. After the short journey from the collieries, the loaded trains were divided and pushed up the washery gradient by single locomotives under full power, or undivided trains were backed up to the washery sidings by engines working in tandem. The Maesteg washery was one of the last places in Britain where groups of steam locomotives were in commercial operation. However, the first diesels eventually arrived in 1973, although the tank engines survived until 1977.

OAKWOOD COLLIERY 1868–1928
NGR SS861906

Oakwood Colliery, also known as Maesteg Merthyr Colliery and Davis's Pit, was sunk in 1868 by William Davis of Bridgend. The early years of the colliery were blighted by a major explosion in January 1872 which claimed eleven lives.

Davis's mining venture traded as Maesteg Merthyr Collieries Ltd from 1874 to 1899 though it is probable that the ownership of the colliery passed from the Davis family to James Barrow and Ebenezer Lewis after the trade depression of the late 1870s. The mine was put up for sale in 1898 and was eventually bought by Sir Alfred Jones of the Elder Dempster shipping company in 1900. Sir Alfred bought the nearby Garth Colliery at the same time. The workings were deepened to the *Bute* seam at 300 yards by the new company which traded as Elder's Navigation Collieries Ltd. Elder's worked the Garth and Oakwood mines as one operation. The photograph below shows the colliery when it was purchased by Elder Dempster & Co. The No.1 Pit is in the centre of the photo with the No.2 Pit in the background, adjacent to Bethania Street. The No.2 Pit was the upcast/ventilation shaft and a Waddle Fan can be seen on the far left. The Maesteg–Bridgend railway line bisected the colliery.

After the death of Sir Alfred Jones in 1909, Elder Dempster retained the ownership of Oakwood, changing the company name to Celtic Collieries Ltd in 1915. A year later the Cambrian Combine bought the company and retained the new name. Oakwood continued in production with a workforce of about 250 until closure in 1928.

General View, 1900. *Inset:* One of Elder's Navigation Collieries' ten-ton coal wagons of the period 1900–1910.

Original **ventilation flue** of 1868 above a furnace located near the bottom of the shaft. Because of the strong up-draught from the furnace-fire, fresh air was drawn down the No.1 shaft, about seventy-five yards away, and through the workings.

Waddle Fan probably installed in the mid 1870s. The fan was driven by an engine in the building to the left. As it revolved, stale air was drawn up through the shaft and expelled through the rim of the fan. This created the up-draught necessary to draw fresh air down the No.1 shaft and through the workings.

No.2 Pit, Oakwood Colliery. Changing Methods of Ventilation.

Above: The Oakwood No.2 Pit, Bethania Street, pictured around 1914.
Below: The former site the No.2 Pit from a similar viewpoint in March 2005. The remainder of the colliery tip was removed in 1974 and a new link road was completed between Bethania Street and the nearby industrial estate.

No.1 Pit, Oakwood Colliery, c.1910 (view from the south-west). No.1 was the 'working pit' at the mine, the No.2 shaft was primarily used for ventilation. Although the workings were deepened by Elder's Navigation during 1901–2, there were few changes on the surface; redevelopment was concentrated at Garth. To the right is a section of the large tip which covered much of the valley floor between Bridgend Road and Bethania Street.

No.1 Pit, 1920, (view from the north-west) under the ownership of Celtic Collieries Ltd. The pit, set in a densely populated part of the valley with its cluster of old buildings around a wooden head frame, formed a marked contrast to the larger, more modern deep mines on the outskirts of the urban area.

Oakwood Colliery: Changing Industrial Landscapes.

Above: Oakwood Colliery, around 1909, under the ownership of Elder's Navigation Collieries Ltd.

Below: A view from a similar position in March 2005. The colliery site and the large adjoining tip were cleared in the late 1940s and early 1950s and Government Advance Factories were built at a lower level on the reclaimed land. Initially three moderately sized units were constructed and, over the last fifty years, the COSi cosmetics plant (formerly Revlon) has grown to dominate the reclaimed colliery site.

ST JOHN'S COLLIERY 1908-1985
NGR SS876917

St John's Colliery was the last major development undertaken by North's Navigation Collieries. The North and South Pits were sunk to the *Lower New (Bute)* seam at 385 yards during the years 1908 to 1910. Throughout its working life St John's was known locally as Cwmdu Colliery as it was developed on the site of an older colliery of that name. With two large deep mines in the northern part of the valley producing mainly steam coal, North's sought to diversify its output and St John's was sunk primarily to develop the lower seams of prime coking coal in the Maesteg/Garth district.

The early years of the colliery were difficult ones due to geological problems. The shafts were sunk close to the crest of the Maesteg anticline so the seams dip to the south in the southern part of the workings and to the north in the northern districts. Due to the dip of the seams and the disturbed nature of the ground, especially in the fractured area known as the 'Jubilee Slide', the underground roadways were subjected to considerable pressures which limited the progress of the mine until 1918.

The colliery prospered in the early 1920s, reaching its peak workforce total of 1,479 in 1920. As the mine supplied a wide range of markets and was not dependent on the steam coal export trade, St John's maintained high employment levels during the trade depression of the late 1920s and early 1930s.

The first years after nationalisation in 1947 were difficult ones. Productivity was low and significant losses were incurred. However, with the development of the *Gelli Deg* seam, which began in 1951, the fortunes of the colliery changed and the mine was soon in profit. The *Gelli Deg* seam ensured the success of St John's through the 1950s and 1960s. In May 1963, for example, 875 tons per day were raised at the South Pit from the *Gelli Deg* and 120 tons per day were produced at the North Pit from the *Seven Feet* seam.

During the mid-1950s there was an extensive modernisation programme at the colliery. The original steam-powered winding engines were replaced, and the engine houses were enlarged to accommodate the new electric winders.

By the late 1970s and early 1980s the bulk of the output of the colliery came from the *Lower Nine Feet (Upper New)*, *Six Feet* and *Gelli Deg* seams. The latter seam was worked-out by 1984, but there were considerable reserves of prime coking coal remaining at the colliery, especially in the *Six Feet* seam.

In 1981 St John's was still regarded as a 'long life' pit but, due largely to the exhaustion of the *Gelli Deg* seam and the geological difficulties that affected production costs, the colliery was 'in crisis' by February 1984. At that time the Coal Board and the miners' representatives agreed that the South Pit reserves were exhausted. After the miners' strike of 1984–5 the future of the mine was again reviewed and, despite the proposals of the NUM to develop the substantial reserves at the colliery, the Coal Board recommended, in April 1985, that St John's should close.

As part of a six-month campaign to keep the mine open, an Independent Public Inquiry chaired by Alan Fisher, a past president of the TUC, was convened in July at County Hall Cardiff, and the key issues relating to the future of the colliery were considered.

The Public Inquiry Panel was of the opinion that the considerable reserves at the mine could be efficiently worked by reducing the workforce from 880 to 450 as an alternative to closure. The panel also considered that the social and economic costs of closure, in an area of limited alternative employment, would be more costly to the government than any programme of financial support for the colliery. However, the mid-1980s saw changing government attitudes to support for the older industrial communities as the Conservative government promoted market economics at the expense of socio-economic considerations. So, despite the determined drive to retain a mining workforce in the district, and the recommendation of the independent inquiry that there was a powerful case for keeping St John's open, the mine ceased production at the end of 1985, thus ending 155 years of commercial mining in the Llynfi Valley.

Repairing the Cwmdu mineral line, with St John's Colliery in the background, in April 1953. The mile-long line originally formed part of the North's Navigation internal railway system that linked the company's Llynfi Valley collieries and connected the mines to the South Wales rail network.

The original winding engine house at the South Pit, before and during enlargement in the mid-1950s.

Opposite: St John's Colliery, *c.*1920, South Pit (upcast) to the left. *Inset:* One of 200 twenty-ton Great Western Railway coal wagons allocated to North's Navigation Collieries in the mid-1920s.

Two views of the North Pit in February 1955 during modernisation.

Above: The two conical tips that were Llynfi Valley landmarks for decades form the backdrop to the original steam-powered winding engine house of 1909.

Below: Preparing to enlarge the engine house to accommodate electric-powered winding equipment.

The North Pit engine house during the modernisation of the colliery in 1955.

The North Pit in 1984, shortly before the closure of the mine. The remnants of the large conical tips, which were lowered and landscaped in the 1970s, are in the background.

Two views of surface activity at St John's Colliery in the 1950s.

Left: Pit pony at work in 1952, towards the end of the era of horse-power in the mines. In 1907 there were 500 ponies at work locally in North's Navigation collieries; by 1973 there were just eighty-five in harness in the deep mines of South Wales.

Below: Part of the original steam winding engine at the North Pit in February 1954. It was made by Fraser and Chalmers; Corliss valve gear is shown to the right. In 1950 there were 177 men employed on the surface at St John's, about 16 per cent of the colliery workforce.

Right: Cwmdu colliers waiting to start a shift at St John's Colliery, May 1963.

Below: The start of an afternoon shift at St John's in 1985.

The end of an era for St John's Colliery and the Llynfi Valley.

Left: Demolition of the South Pit headgear in January 1986, just one month after the closure of the colliery.

Below: Filling the South Pit shaft in January 1986.

Other Collieries and Mine-Workings I

In addition to the seven large mines in production in the Llynfi Valley during the twentieth century, there were also a number of other collieries in operation during the years 1830–85. The two largest mines in this earlier group were the Gin Pit and the nearby Dyffryn Madoc Pit. In 1863, 163 were employed at the Gin Pit, and, in 1878, 400 worked at Dyffryn Madoc. The latter colliery was one of the first mines in South Wales to have coal washing equipment on-site when a processing plant was installed there by Sheppard & Sons of Bridgend in the mid-1870s. The Gin Pit was the scene of the most serious mining accident in the Llynfi Valley when eleven men and three boys were killed in an explosion on Boxing Day 1863. The Gin Pit ceased production in 1875 and Dyffryn Madoc closed in 1878.

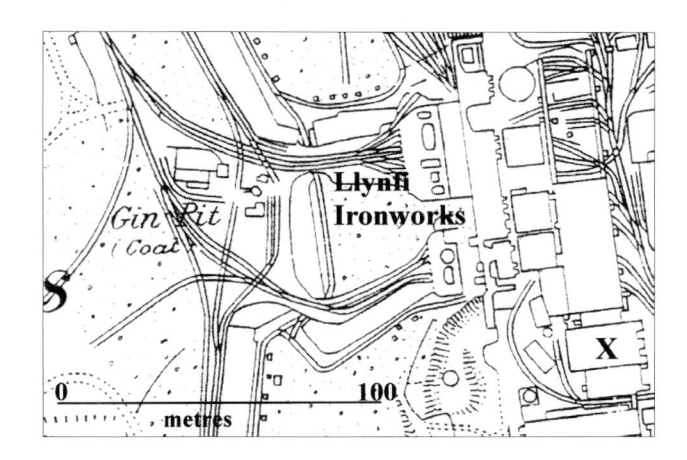

Map view of the upcast shaft at the Gin Pit in the mid-1870s. The pit was located on the Llynfi Ironworks site adjoining the coke ovens on higher ground above the blast furnaces.

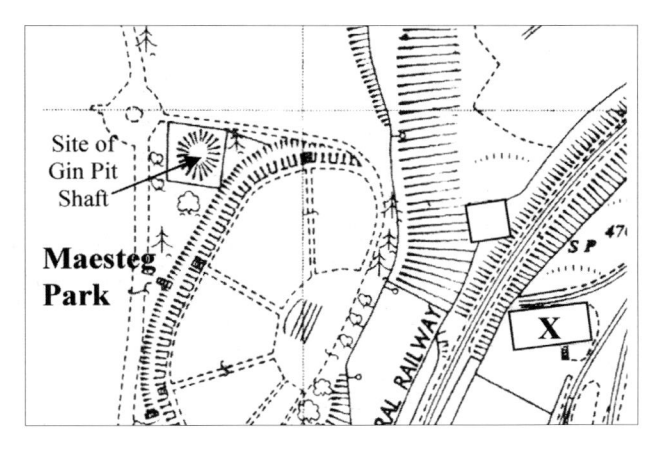

Map view of the same area in the 1940s after much of the ironworks site had been redeveloped as a welfare park. The abandoned Gin Pit shaft is shown in a fenced-off corner above the 'arena' of Maesteg Park. The building marked 'X' on both maps is now the reception area of the Maesteg Sports Centre.

Other Collieries and Mine-Workings II

Before the sinking of the Coegnant deep mine during 1881–3, the most important collieries in the Coegnant district were the levels at Tygwyn-bach and Tywith. The mines were just 700m apart, both worked similar coal and black-band ironstone seams and both collieries were linked to local ironworks. Tywith originally supplied the Tondu Works, Tygwyn-bach was associated with the Llynfi Works in Maesteg. The latter mine was also known as the No.11 Level. Both collieries closed in 1884, although Tygwyn-bach was later re-opened as a 'small mine'.

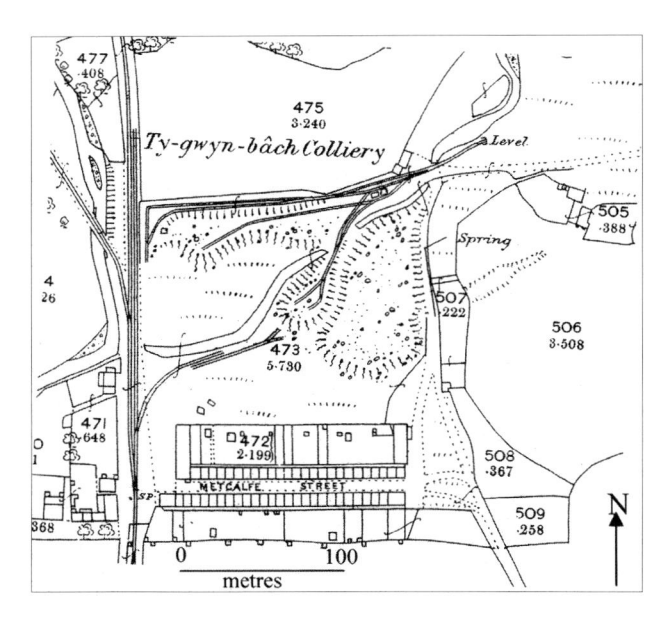

The Tygwyn-bach Level in the 1870s. The mine was opened up near the outcrop of the *Caedefaid* seam. Nearby Metcalfe Street was built to house the Llynvi Iron Co.'s coal and ironstone miners in the Coegnant district.

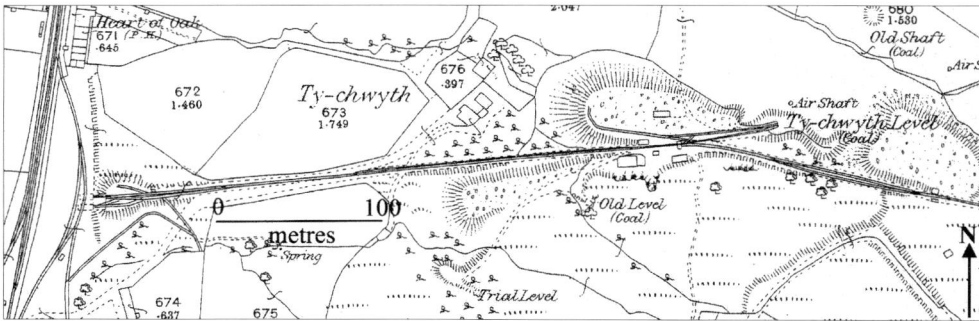

Tywith (Ty-chwyth) Level, pictured around 1876. The level was originally opened in 1846, also near the outcrop of the *Caedefaid* seam. It was the main local iron ore source for the Tondu Ironworks producing 15,000 tons of black-band ironstone for the Tondu furnaces in 1859.

Other Collieries and Mine-Workings III

There were also a number of small levels in the Coegnant and Caerau districts, although there is very little contemporary information available about them. The largest was probably Dyffryn Colliery which was located on the hillside about 400m to the north-west of the Navigation Hotel in Caerau. It was connected to the railway system in the valley by an incline plane. A short distance to the south-west, the original Dyffryn Rhondda Colliery, with its associated brick works, was opened in the late 1870s. The mine closed in November 1882 due to faulting, and it is not clear if the colliery was ever in full production again. From a contemporary plan in the Great Western Railway Archives, there was a Dyffryn Rhondda Colliery siding, with screens, near the present-day Caerau Square in the late 1870s. However, it is not clear how the coal reached the siding from the colliery. Both levels probably worked the *No.2 Rhondda (Wernddu)* seam. The Dyffryn Rhondda name was later applied to the large deep mine in the Afan Valley, about one mile to the north of the original level, which was in production from 1904 to 1966. Two other significant mines were the Yard and Victoria levels near Tywith Colliery in the Coegnant district.

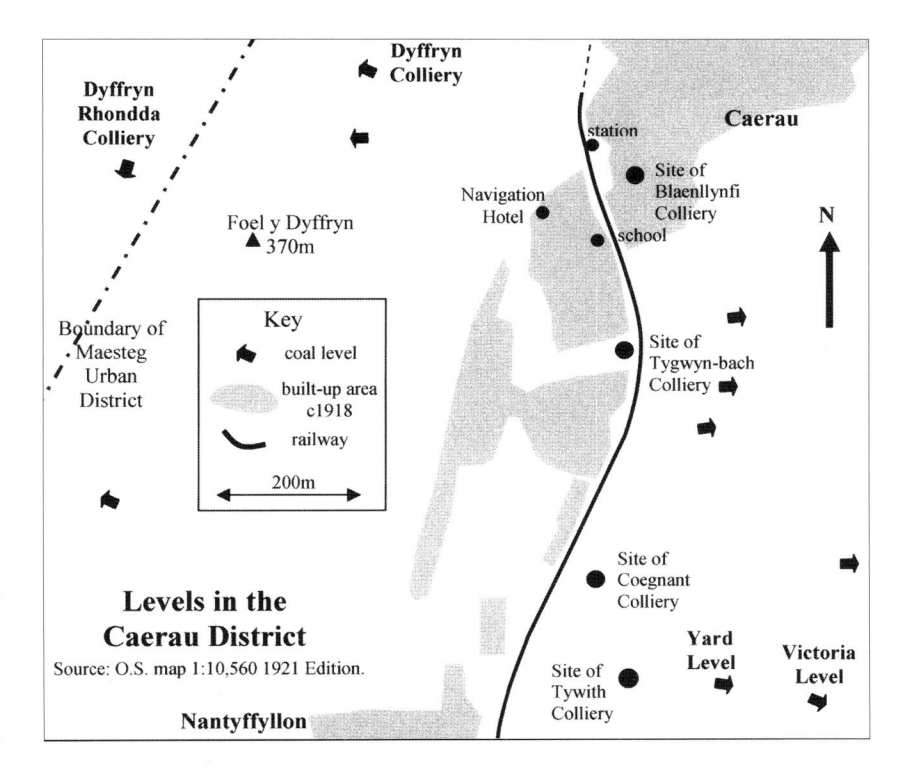

Levels in the Caerau district.
Source: OS map 1:10,560 1921 edition

Other Collieries and Mine-Workings IV

'Open-cast' or 'patch' workings in the mid-1870s, in the area immediately to the north-east of the present-day South Parade Playing Fields. The *Four Feet* and *Six Feet* coking coal seams and also iron ore 'pins' were probably mined from these extensive open pits with their networks of tramways. In 2003–4 the site was reclaimed before redevelopment as the site of a comprehensive school and housing.

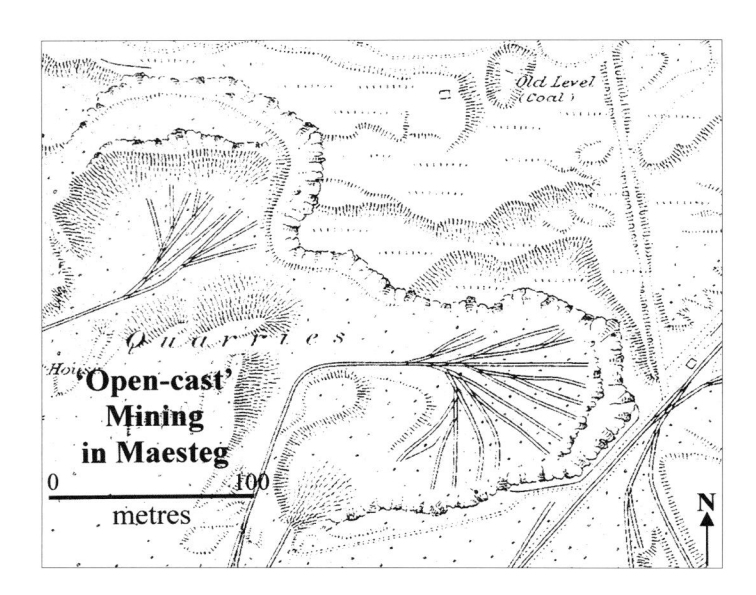

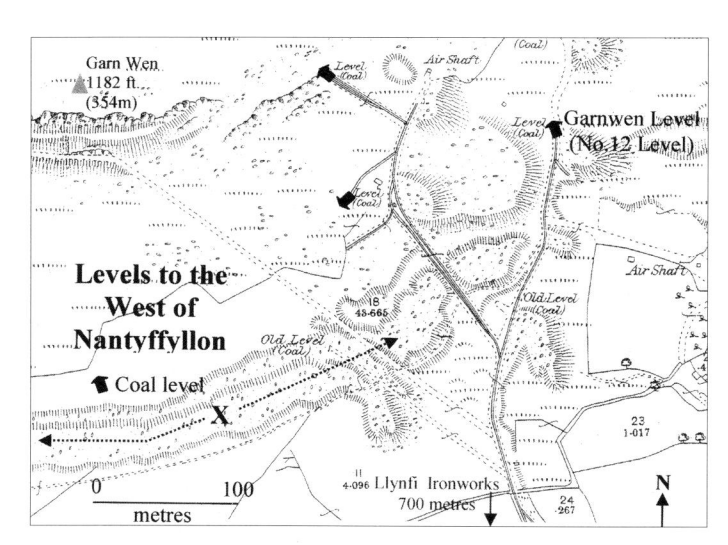

The southern slope of Garn Wen was intensively mined during the period 1850–85. On this OS map, drawn-up in the mid-1870s, there are a number of levels and trench-workings connected to the Llynfi Ironworks by a network of tramways with incline planes. The coal levels worked the *White* and *Clay* seams near the intersection of the Upper and Middle Coal Measures. Also black-band ironstone for the Llynfi Works was mined from the large surface excavation at 'X'.

Other Collieries and Mine-Workings V

The seams worked on the slopes of Garn Wen also outcropped 3km to the southeast in the Garth district. The western slope of Garth Hill was intensively mined by the Patent Galvanized Iron Co. in the mid-nineteenth century to supply coking coal and iron ore to that company's short-lived ironworks at Garth. Most of the levels shown in the illustration below worked the *Clay* and *White* seams. The workings included a pit shaft near Caergymrig Farm which was possibly the first in the Maesteg district.

Towards the end of the nineteenth century the emphasis shifted to deep-mining in the district with the development of Garth Colliery, although a number of levels were still in production on a small scale in the early twentieth century. For example, in 1908, Elder's Navigation operated the Garth Level with just six workers, and a Celtic Lower Level was listed under the ownership of Celtic Collieries with a workforce of thirty-three at the time of closure (around 1928).

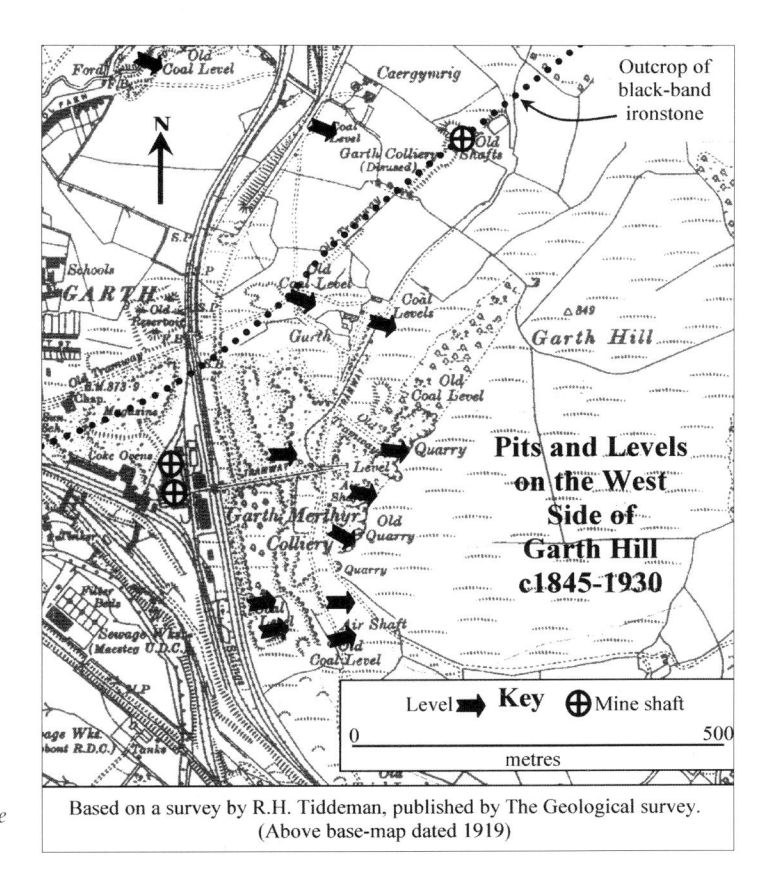

Pits and levels on the west side of Garth Hill, 1845–1930. *Source: Based on a survey by R.H. Tiddeman, published by the Geological survey*

Other Collieries and Mine-Workings VI

As well as the major collieries operating in the Llynfi Valley during the years 1830–1985 and the levels already noted, there were at least twenty small mines in production around the town centre of Maesteg. The largest group was located to the north-east of the built-up area. Most of the small mines employed less than ten workers although some employed up to forty miners. For example the Quarry (or Oakwood) Level, at the head of the old 'Coed Quarry', (No.1 on the map) employed twenty-nine workers underground in 1918, and two on the surface. Other small mines were the Coed Level (No.2) near the top of Park Street, and Bryn Rhyg Colliery (No.3) near Maesteg Cemetery, which was known to local wags as 'The Spirit Level'. The latter mine employed eleven workers at the time of closure (around 1928).

In total there were at least sixty collieries and sizeable commercial levels in operation in the Llynfi Valley at various times during the years 1830–1985.

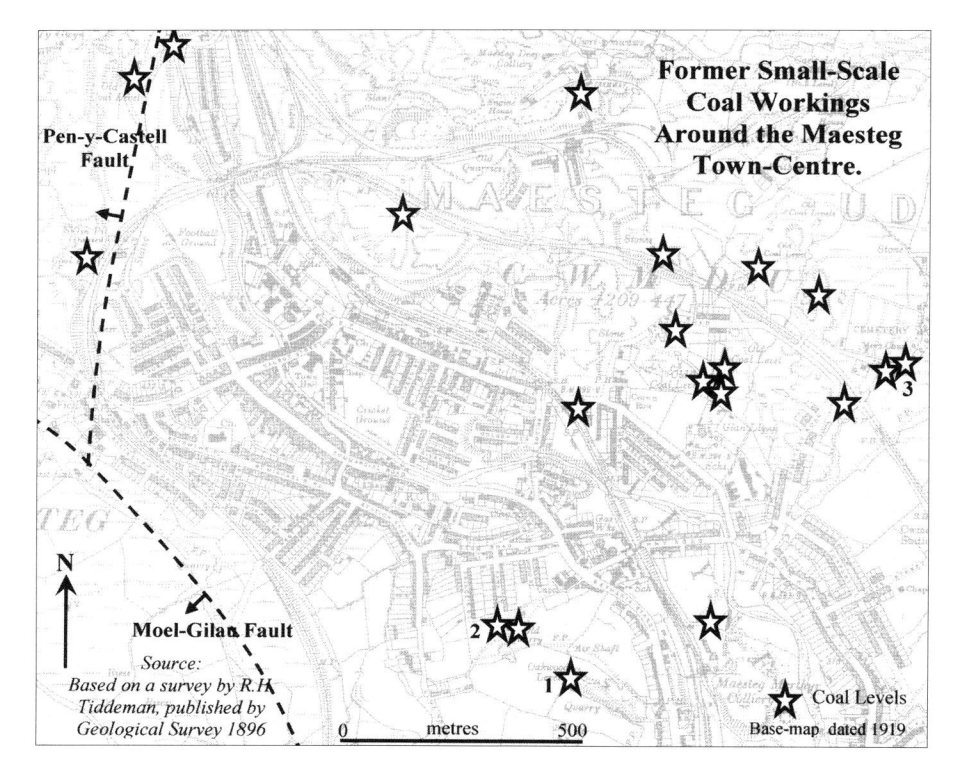

Former small-scale coal workings around the Maesteg town centre. *Source: Based on a survey by R.H. Tiddeman, published by the Geological survey 1896*

PART THREE

FOR REFERENCE

THE ORIGINAL ADMIRALTY LIST OF SOUTH WALES STEAM COALS 1904

Albion Merthyr	Cambrian Navigation
Cory's Merthyr	Cyfarthfa
Dowlais Cardiff	Dowlais Merthyr
Ferndale	Great Western Navigation
Harris's Deep Navigation	Hill's Plymouth Merthyr
Hood's Merthyr	Insole's Merthyr
Lewis's Merthyr	Locket's Merthyr
Maclaren Merthyr	National Merthyr
Naval Merthyr	Nixon's Navigation
North's Imperial Navigation	Ocean Merthyr
Oriental Merthyr	Penrikyber
Powell Dyffryn	Rhymney
Standard Merthyr	Ynysfeio

AGENCIES SUPPLIED WITH STEAM COAL BY NORTH'S NAVIGATION COLLIERIES (1889) LTD, 1912–16

Austrian Lloyds Steam Navigation Co.
Deutsche Kohlen-Depot
The French Navy
HM Government
The Italian Navy
Italian State Railways
The Russian Navy
The Tug Coaling Syndicate
The Union Castle Mail Steamship Co.

SS *Elmina* (4,798 tons), a typical example of the large number of Elder Dempster steamers supplied with bunker fuel from the shipping company's Llynfi Valley collieries, 1900–16.

Llynfi Valley Collieries: Employment Totals for Selected Years, 1891–1976

Colliery	1891	1896	1897	1899	1907	1910	1914	1920	1922	1924	1925
Caerau	137	533	812	862	1699	2131	2403	2392	2432	2388	2124
Coegnant	586	569	701	812	1760	1926	2182	1942	1933	1914	1961
St John's	—	—	—	—	—	391	670	1479	1380	1473	1324
Maesteg Deep	40	156	275	366	604	671	671	546	146	277	283
Number Nine	350	353	393	246	255	—	—	—	—	—	—
Oakwood	249	391	347	495	123	239	246	226	237	275	275
Garth	535	504	445	468	1001	411	740	742	670	753	749
Totals	**1897**	**2506**	**2973**	**3249**	**5442**	**5769**	**6912**	**7327**	**6798**	**7080**	**6716**

Colliery	1930	1931	1933	1934	1935	1936	1945	1948	1950	1962	1976
Caerau	1585	469	42	384	345	455	586	686	825	652	529
Coegnant	1400	691	1032	1099	1039	1155	722	710	651	828	752
St John's	1180	1223	1298	1351	1374	1339	1142	1162	1082	856	811
Maesteg Deep	139	—	—	—	—	—	—	—	—	—	—
Garth	639	—	—	—	—	—	—	—	—	—	—
Totals	**4943**	**2383**	**2372**	**2834**	**2758**	**2949**	**2450**	**2558**	**2558**	**2336**	**2092**

Colliery Ownership 1864–1947

Caerau: NNC 1890 to nationalisation in 1947.

Coegnant: L&TCo 1881–89, NNC 1889 to 1947.

Garth: John Brogden & Sons 1864–72, LTOC&ICo 1872–78, Rec. 1878–80, Garth Merthyr Steam Navigation Collieries Ltd 1883–99, VIC 1899–1900, ENC 1900–1910, Elder's Collieries Ltd 1910–15, Celtic Collieries Ltd 1915–1930.

Maesteg Deep: Llynvi Coal & Iron Co. Ltd 1868–72, LTOC&ICo 1872–78, Rec. 1878–80, L&TCo 1880–89, NNC 1889–1930.

Number Nine: Llynvi Coal & Iron Co. Ltd 1867–72, LTOC&ICo 1872–78, Rec. 1878–80, L&TCo 1880–89, NNC 1889–1908.

Oakwood: Wm. Davis & Son 1868–74, Maesteg Merthyr Collieries Ltd 1874–99, VIC 1899–1900, ENC 1900–1910, Elder's Collieries Ltd 1910–15, Celtic Collieries Ltd 1915–28.

St John's: NNC 1908–1947.

Years of Closure:

Number Nine-1908, Oakwood-1928, Maesteg Deep-1930, Garth-1930, Caerau-1977, Coegnant-1981, St John's-1985

Abbreviations Used:

ENC	Elder's Navigation Collieries Ltd
LTOC&ICo	Llynvi Tondu & Ogmore Coal & Iron Co. Ltd
L&TCo	Llynvi & Tondu Co. Ltd
NNC	North's Navigation Collieries (1889) Ltd
Rec	in Receivership
VIC	Victoria Investment Corporation

Sources: Mines Dept. List of Mines, 1891–1950, Colliery Guardian: Guide to the Coalfields, 1962, 1976

Llynfi Valley Collieries Associated with the Local Iron Industry, 1854–84

Year	Name of Colliery *	Name of Owner	Notes
1854	Llynvi Works Maesteg Works	Llynvi Vale Iron Co. R.P. Lemon & Co.	
1856	Llynvi Works Maesteg Works Cwmdu Tywith	Llynvi Vale Iron Co. R.P. Lemon & Co. Charles Sheppard John Brogden & Sons	Cwmdu opened 1856, Tywith originally opened by Sir Robert Price of Tondu Ironworks in 1846, re-opened 1856.
1862	Llynvi Works Maesteg Works Cwmdu (I) Cwmdu (II) Tywith	Llynvi Vale Iron Co. " John Brogden & Sons " "	Maesteg Works bought-up by Llynvi Vale Iron Co. in 1862. The Brogdens opened a new level at Cwmdu in 1860 and bought an existing level at Cwmdu in 1861.
1871	Gin Pit Dyffryn Madoc Pit No.5 Level No.8 Level No.9 Level (Caedefaid Colliery) No.11 Level (Tygwynbach Colliery) Moffatt's Level Cwmdu (I) Cwmdu (II) Garth Colliery Tywith Colliery	Llynvi Coal & Iron Co. Ltd " " " " " " John Brogden & Sons " " "	Levels 5 and 8 closed in 1873, Gin Pit closed 1875. No.9 Level was opened-up in 1867, and Moffatt's Level dates from 1868. The Brogdens sunk the Garth Pit in 1864. Blaenllynfi Colliery not listed.
1877	Dyffryn Madoc Pit No.9 Level No.11 Level No. 12 Level (Garnwen Colliery) Maesteg Deep Colliery Tywith Colliery Cwmdu Garth Colliery	Llynvi Tondu & Ogmore C&I Co. " " " " " " "	Dyffryn Madoc not listed after 1878, Garnwen first listed 1872. Only one Cwmdu level was listed after 1871. Moffatt's Level was redeveloped as Maesteg Deep Colliery in the early 1870s. Garth not listed 1877–82, re-opened 1883, closed 1930.
1883	No.9 Level No. 11 Level (Tygwynbach Colliery) No.12 Level (Garnwen Colliery) Cwmdu Maesteg Deep Colliery Tywith Colliery Coegnant Colliery	Llynvi & Tondu Co. " " " " " "	No.9 remained in production until 1908 and Maesteg Deep until 1930. Coegnant was opened in 1882 and closed in 1981. The other three collieries closed in 1884, although Cwmdu and Tygwynbach were later re-opened as small levels.

Sources: a) Hunt's Mineral Statistics and b) Mines Department List of Mines *Before 1871 the Mineral Statistics did not include the names of individual collieries owned by the larger iron companies.

Coal Exports from Port Talbot 1904 and 1912

	1904	1904	1912	1912
Region	Tonnage Exported	Percentage of Total	Tonnage Exported	Percentage of Total
Hamburg – Brest	27,230	4.22	232,263	15.32
W. France	157,547	24.40	544,165	35.89
N. Spain & Portugal	49,539	7.67	52,827	3.48
Mediterranean	67,138	10.41	271,615	17.91
W. Africa	60,163	9.34	37,255	2.45
Pacific N. & S. America	180,687	28.01	242,367	15.98
Other regions	102,894	15.95	136,040	8.97
Total	**645,204**	**100.00**	**1,516,013**	**100.00**

Ports Importing Coal from Port Talbot 1904 and 1912

	1904	1904	1912	1912
Port	Tonnage Exported	Percentage of Total	Tonnage Exported	Percentage of Total
Bordeaux, France	31,645	4.9	210,300	13.9
Zeebrugge, Belgium	0	0	146,470	9.7
Genoa, Italy	48,795	7.6	136,942	9.0
Valparaiso, Chile	0	0	87,161	5.7
St Nazaire, France	35,601	5.5	80,352	5.3
La Rochelle, France	0	0	72,729	4.8
Nantes, France	46,826	7.2	63,519	4.2
Bayonne, France	0	0	52,719	3.5
Iquique, Chile	73,366	11.4	43,640	2.9
Antofagasta, Chile	0	0	43,574	2.9

Sources: South Wales Coal Annual, *1905, 1913*

After the opening of its railway and new docks in 1897, Port Talbot became the main port of export for the Llynfi Valley collieries. The above tables give an indication of the foreign markets supplied with Llynfi Valley coal.

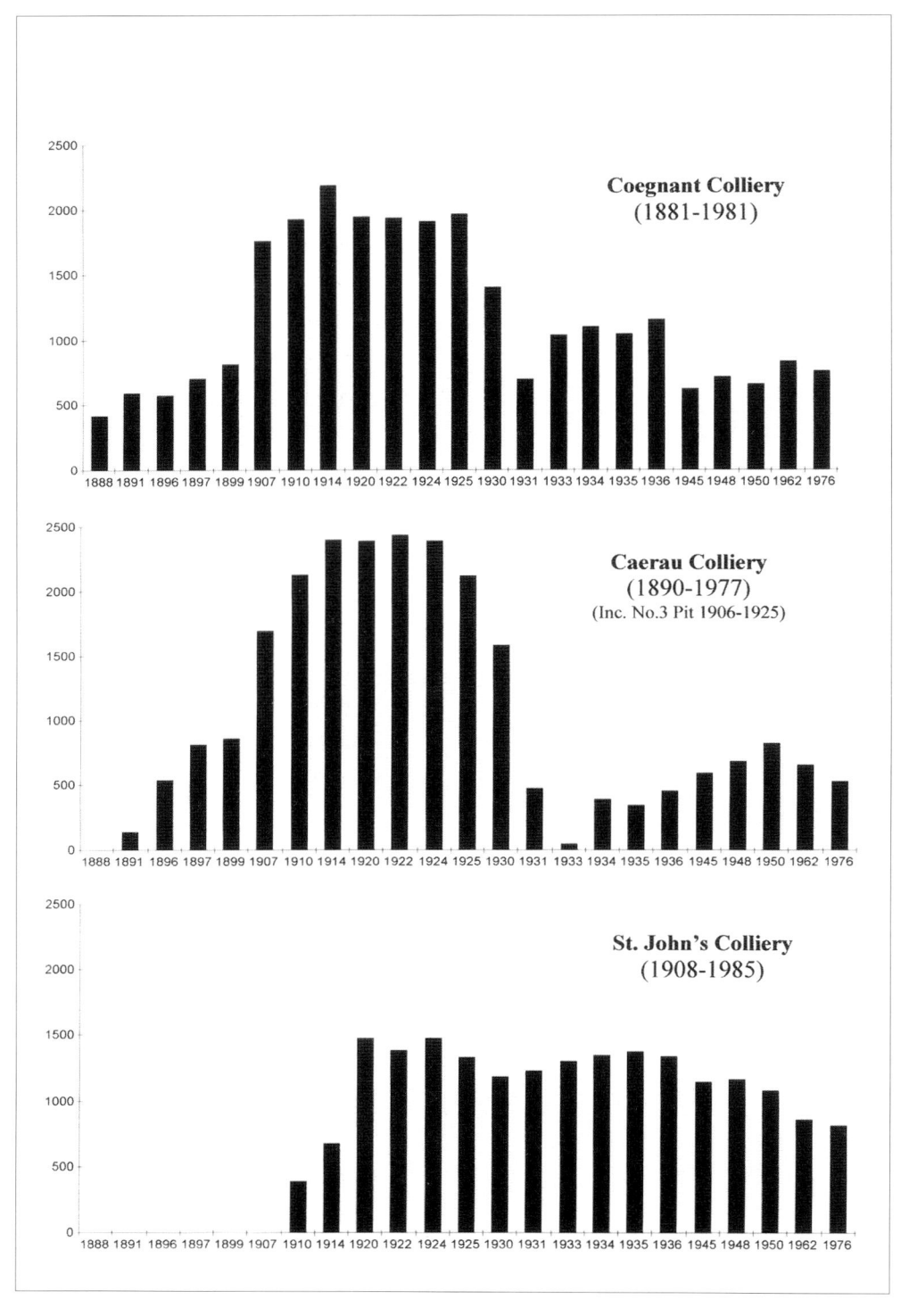

Graphs showing employment totals at three Llynfi Valley collieries for selected years. *Source: Report of HM Inspectors of Mines, 1888 HMSO; Mines Dept List of Mines, 1891–1950 HMSO;* Colliery Guardian, *Guide to the Coalfields 1962, 1976*

Sailings from Port Talbot with local coal for Iquique, Chile, during the first six months of 1905

Ship	Owner (where known)	Cleared Port	Cargo, tons
Rancagua	A.D. Bordes, Dunkirk	Jan. 12	2,750
Melpomene	B. Wencke-Söhne, Hamburg	Jan. 13	2,800
Mneme	B. Wencke-Söhne, Hamburg	Jan. 20	2,323
Atlantique	A.D. Bordes, Dunkirk	Jan. 20	3,500
Hera	B. Wencke-Söhne, Hamburg	Jan. 20	3,500
Quillota	A.D. Bordes, Dunkirk	Jan. 28	2,800
Terpsichore		Feb. 1	3,200
Kalliope		Feb. 3	2,800
Hebe	B. Wencke-Söhne, Hamburg	Feb. 23	3,910
Grace Harwar	W. Montgomery, London	Mar. 1	3,000
Reine Blanche	A.D. Bordes, Dunkirk	Mar. 4	2,400
Nord	A.D. Bordes, Dunkirk	Mar. 8	4,500
Archibald Russell	John Hardy & Sons, Glasgow	Mar. 17	3,900
Croissett	Leroux & Co., Rouen	Mar. 24	2,000
Kurt	G. Siemers, Hamburg	Apr. 14	5,000
Cap Horn	A.D. Bordes, Dunkirk	Apr. 15	4,000
Wega		May 1	3,194
Peru		May 5	3,250
Meridian		May 5	2,650
Melete	B. Wencke-Söhne, Hamburg	May 5	2,700
Walkure		May 16	2,650
Edmund		May 24	4,700
Ben Lee		June 5	3,788
Cavaliere Ciampa		June 10	2,600
Gunford	Briggs & Co., Glasgow	June 14	3,600
Norma		June 19	3,470
Aldebaran		June 23	2,830
Rigel		June 23	1,879

Source: Cardiff Shipping and Mercantile Gazette, Jan–Jun 1905

These vessels were among the largest sailing ships in the world at that time and many were owned by the famous French firm of A.D. Bordes. The voyages around Cape Horn to the Pacific coast of South America, lasted up to three-and-a-half months.

Coal Exports from South Wales to Chile, 1903-4: 421.804 tons

Source: South Wales Coal Annual, 1903, 1904.

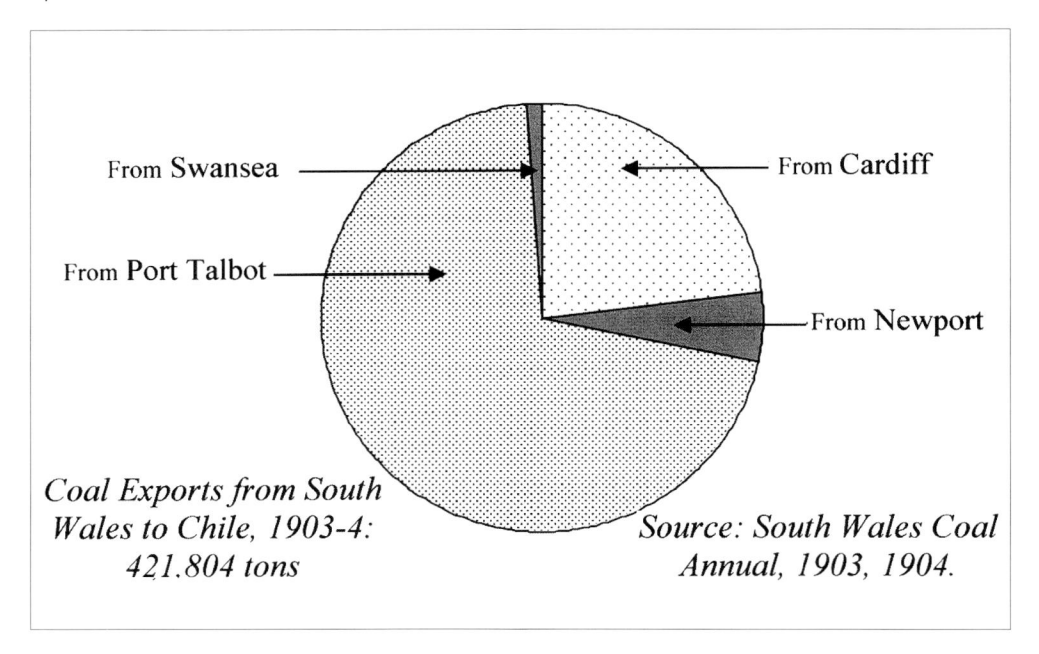

North's Navigation Collieries and the coal trade with Chile 1903–5. Because of the link between North's collieries and the nitrate industry, Chile became an important market for South Wales coal during the early years of the twentieth century, and Port Talbot was by far the most important port of export to the nitrate lands.

COLLIERIES	Where Situated	Port Talbot exclusive of tipping	Cardiff exclusive of tipping	Barry exclusive of tipping	Swansea exclusive of tipping
	Port Talbot Rly.	d.			
Duffryn Rhondda	Bryn	6	2/1	2/1	⎫
Bryn Navigation	,,	6	2/1	2/1	⎬ 1/0½
Cefn-y-Bryn	,,	6	2/1	2/1	⎭
Tonhir	Maesteg	6½	2/3	2/3	1/1
North's Navigation Collieries	,,	7	1/4	1/2	1/1
Tygwynbach	,,	7	1/4	1/2	1/1
Garth	,,	8	1/4	1/2	1/2

Comparative rates upon coal to Port Talbot, Cardiff, Barry, and Swansea for shipment. *Source: Port Talbot Railway & Docks Co., Handbook of Rates, 1913*

Local Geology and Mining I

Local geological structures were key factors in the development of the coal industry in the upper Llynfi Valley. Two features in particular, the Maesteg section of the Maesteg-Pontypridd Anticline and the Moel Gilau Fault, were significant locally. On the diagram below, the crest of the anticline (or upfold) in the coal measures is shown at 'A'. The upfold brought a series of valuable coal seams closer to the surface in the Maesteg district. The seams, from the *Two Feet Nine* to the *Gelli Deg*, provided the bulk of the coal mined in the Llynfi Valley after about 1885. Due to the upfold, some of the best seams in South Wales also outcropped in the local area. The famous *Six Feet* seam for example, which was generally deep-mined in the coalfield valleys, was worked by open-cast methods during the nineteenth century in the Maesteg area.

As the rocks were slowly uplifted and folded, stresses created fractures or faults that displaced the most valuable seams in the Maesteg district. In the case of the Moel Gilau fracture, the seams were displaced over 600m along the west side of the Llynfi Valley, placing them beyond the range of conventional mining techniques.

The less resistant rocks of the Middle Coal Measures were exposed by the anticline and were more easily worn down, or eroded. The erosion formed a 'breach' in the mountains to the west of Maesteg which was made use of by the builders of the Maesteg–Port Talbot road during the 1920s.

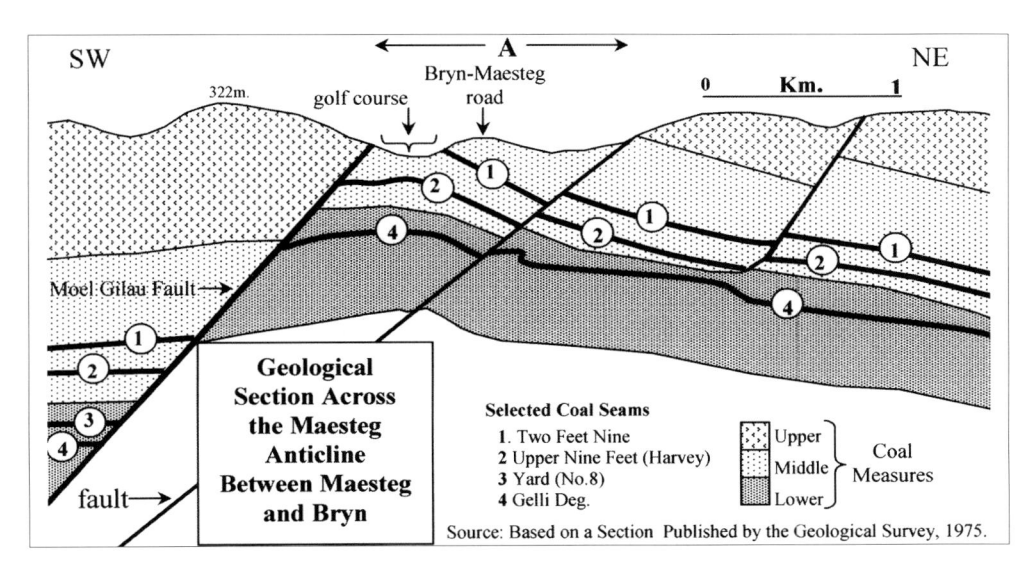

Geological section across the Maesteg anticline between Maesteg and Bryn.

Local Geology and Mining II

Geological conditions in the folded and fractured South Wales Coalfield presented considerable problems for colliers and mining engineers. In the Maesteg area, in addition to the widespread occurrence of local faults, the zone of geological disturbance known as the 'Jubilee Slide' was an area of particular difficulty. The Jubilee Slide is a zone with numerous faults and fractures that affected mining operations over a large section of the coalfield from Gilfach Goch in the east to Pontrhydyfen in the west. The geological evidence suggests that the disturbed strata of the slide was the result of a major rotational landslip that took place during the formation of the Coal Measures.

In the Llynfi Valley, mining operations to the north-east of the Maesteg town centre, between Coegnant and St John's collieries, were severely limited by the Jubilee Slide (see diagrams below). The area marked 'X' on the section was the most seriously affected. In that zone, the valuable seams from the *Six Feet* to the *Lower Nine Feet* could not be traced or were unworkable. The seams above the *Six Feet* and below the *Bute* were less seriously affected.

The other major zone of disturbance, along the Moel Gilau fault already referred to, extends from Blackmill in the east to Swansea Bay in the west. In the Maesteg district it can be traced from Cwmfelin along the western slopes of the Llynfi Valley to Bryn. The coal seams are displaced 650m (2,100ft) to the south-west of the fault. For example, seams which are close to the surface in Llwydarth Road, near Brick Row, are 2,000ft deeper a short distance away, across the fault, near the Cross Inn, Cwmfelin. Due to the Moel Gilau fault, deep-mining operations in the Llynfi Valley were confined to the north and east of a line traced along Neath Road and the A4063 to Cwmfelin.

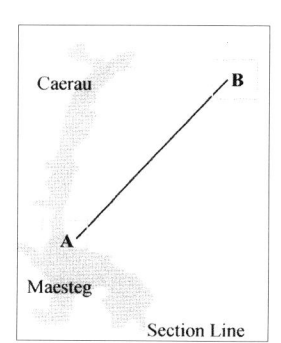

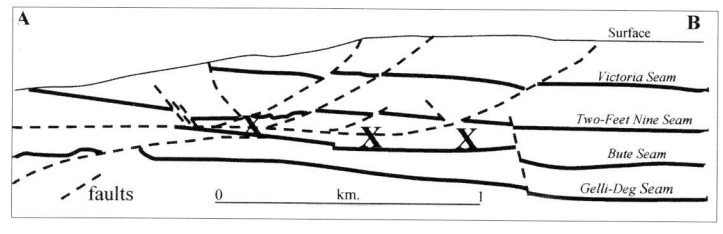

The Jubilee Slide. *Source:* The Geology of the South Wales Coalfield, Part IV, *Woodland and Evans, 1964*

Local Geology and Mining III

The Llynfi Valley collieries produced such a wide variety of coals in such a small section of the coalfield for the reasons shown on the map below. The types, or ranks, of coal occur in bands across the coalfield, and some mining districts developed within just one of the bands, for example, the Mountain Ash area specialised in the production of dry steam coal. The bands narrow towards the west until, in the Maesteg district, the five coal ranks that extend for 16km between Mountain Ash and Caerphilly are compressed into a zone just 5km wide between Maesteg and Cymer Afan. As a result, Caerau Colliery was able to access the higher quality Admiralty steam coals in the north of the valley, and the other collieries in the district could produce high-quality coking and house coals as well as good quality steam descriptions. For similar reasons the Garw Valley could also produce a wide range of coals.

Thus within a 3km radius of Coegnant Colliery, because of the distribution of the ranks of coal, an 'original' Admiralty steam coal was produced at Caerau (North's Imperial Navigation) and another Admiralty coal (Celtic) was mined to the south of the Caerau Pits. In addition, the coking coal of the Maesteg district produced some of the best foundry coke on the market, and Maesteg Deep Colliery and Garth Colliery produced what was regarded as the best house coal in South Wales.

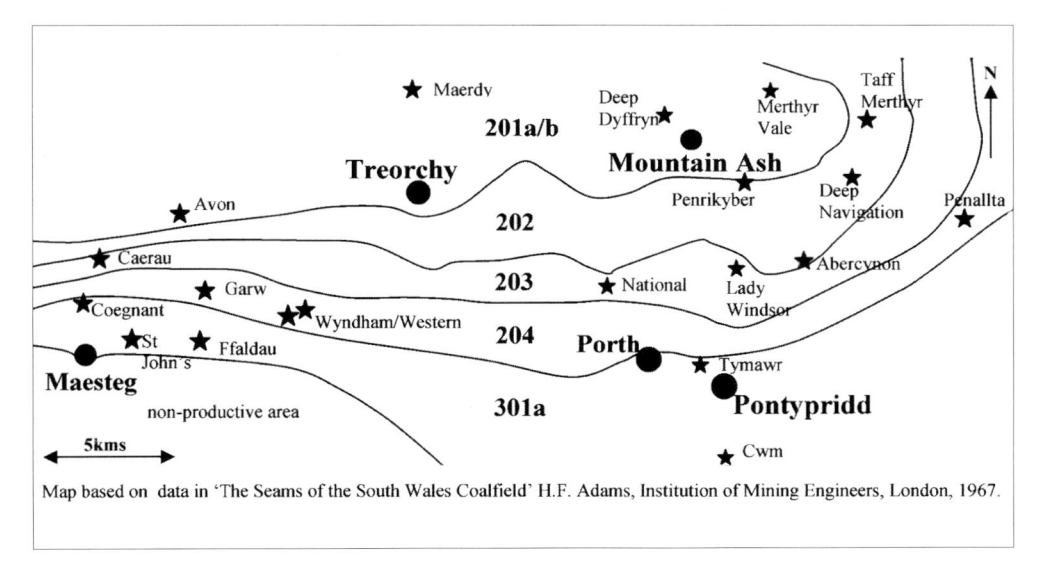

Generalised map to show ranks of coal with collieries from about 1967. Coal rank code: 201a/b dry steam, 202 coking steam (weakly caking), 203 coking steam (medium caking), 204 coking steam (strongly caking), 301a prime coking.

Shaft Sections

In the illustration below the tops of the shaft columns mark the heights of the collieries above sea-level; Garth and Oakwood were located on the valley floor. The two oldest mines, Dyffryn Madoc and the Gin Pit, were relatively small collieries working fairly shallow seams during the years 1850–78. The three largest mines, Caerau, Coegnant and St John's would be further deepened in later years. The St John's section includes a reference to some of the geological difficulties which limited the progress of the colliery during the years 1911–18.

The section from the sinkers' log on page 145 shows the strata and coal seams encountered during the sinking of the North Pit from October 1881 to June 1883. The seams vary from the thin *Coal Tar* vein to the high-quality steam coals of the *Six Feet* and *Seven Feet* seams. The pit was initially sunk to work the latter two seams.

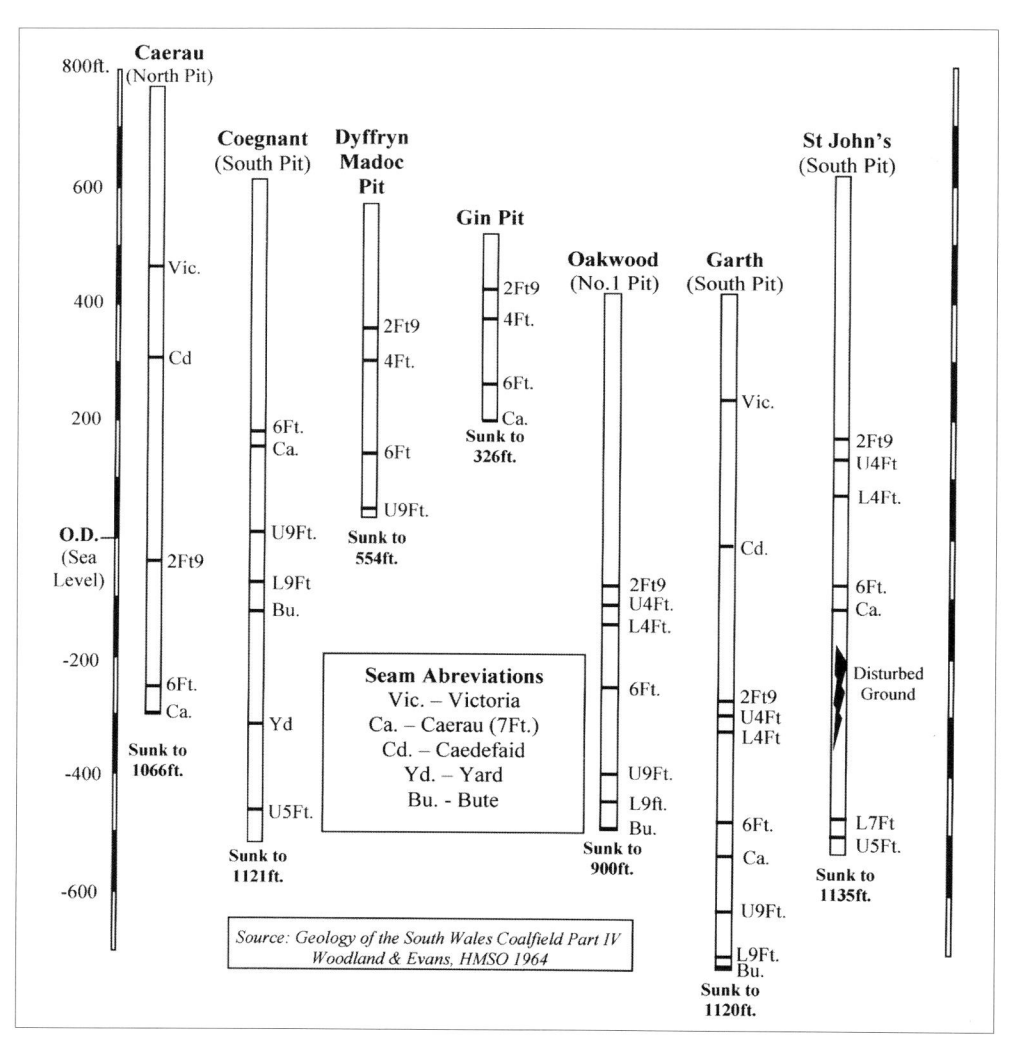

Shaft sections, 1920.

The inset on the right highlights some of the characteristics of Llynfi Valley coal seams. Rarely were there level seams of 'clean' coal. In the example below the *Four Feet* seam is divided into four sections within an overall thickness of about 12ft. The coal also has a significant dip. The main 'parting' in the seam, which was about 3ft at Coegnant, was about 50ft thick further south at the Garth and Oakwood collieries. Thus at those collieries the *Four Feet* was worked as two separate seams: the *Upper Four Feet* and the *Truro (or Lower Four Feet)*.

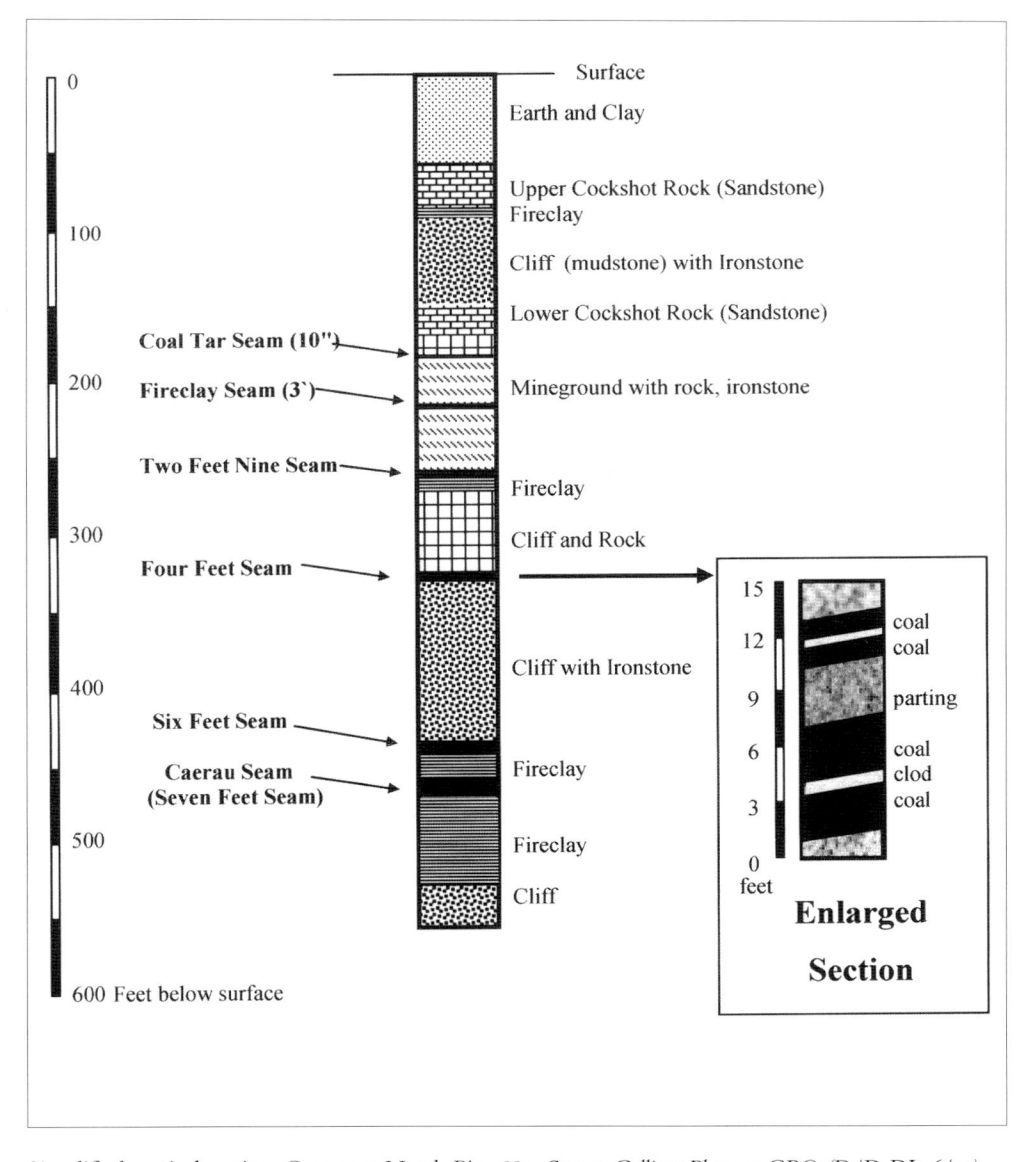

Simplified vertical section, Coegnant North Pit, 1884. *Source: Colliery Plans at GRO (D/D DJ 26/29)*

Colliery Reference Grid

Colliery	Dates (From commencement of sinking)	Maximum Workforce	Shaft Details	Seams Worked	Types of coal produced
Caedefaid (No.9 Level)	1867-1908	403 (1888)	—	Victoria, Caedefaid, Two and a Half.	Coking Coal, House Coal, Steam Coal
Caerau North & South Pits (inc. No.3 Pit 1906-25)	1890-1977	2,432 (1922)	South Pit upcast/ventilation, N. Pit, S. Pit diameters, 20ft No.3 Pit 16ft	Victoria, Two and a Half, Caedefaid, (No.3 Pit); Six Feet, Caerau, Upper Nine Feet, Lower Nine Feet, Bute, Five Feet.	Steam Coal. (North & South Pits). House Coal, Coking Coal (No.3 Pit)
Coegnant North & South Pits	1881-1981	2,182 (1914)	North Pit upcast/ventilation, 15ft diameter, South Pit 20ft	Two Feet Nine, Six Feet, Upper Nine Feet, Lower Nine Feet, Bute, Yard, Seven Feet, Five Feet, Gelli Deg.	Steam Coal, House Coal, Coking Coal
Garth North & South Pits	c1864-1930	1,001 (1907)	North Pit upcast/ventilation, 12ft diameter, South Pit 14ft	Victoria, Upper Yard, Caedefaid, Two Feet Nine, Upper/Lower Four Feet, Six Feet, Caerau, Upper Nine Feet, Lower Nine Feet, Bute.	House Coal, Coking Coal, Steam Coal
Maesteg Deep (Drift Mine)	1868-1930	671 (1910)	(Intake Airway: 7ft 9in x 10ft Return Airway: 8ft 3in x 8ft 3in)	Two Feet Nine Four Feet	House Coal, Coking Coal, Steam Coal
Oakwood No.1 & No.2 Pits	1868-1928	495 (1899)	No.2 Pit upcast/ventilation, No.1 Pit elliptical shaft 16ft x 12ft	Two Feet Nine, Upper/Lower Four Feet, Six Feet, Caerau, Upper Nine Feet, Lower Nine Feet, Bute.	Coking Coal, House Coal., Steam Coal
St John's North & South Pits	1908-1985	1,479 (1920)	South Pit upcast/ventilation, 18ft diameter, North Pit 18ft	Two Feet Nine, Six Feet, Upper Nine Feet, Lower Nine Feet, Bute, Yard, Seven Feet, Five Feet, Gelli Deg.	Coking Coal, Steam Coal, House Coal

Company advertisements, Garth and Oakwood Collieries, from 1923 (top), 1926 (middle) and 1905 (bottom).

LLYNFI VALLEY COLLIERIES: SALES AGENTS 1888–1930

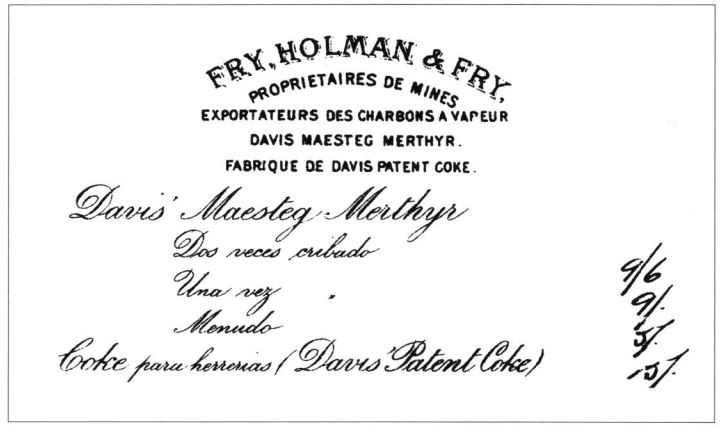

> **FRY, HOLMAN & FRY**
> PROPRIETAIRES DE MINES
> EXPORTATEURS DES CHARBONS A VAPEUR
> DAVIS MAESTEG MERTHYR.
> FABRIQUE DE DAVIS PATENT COKE.
>
> Davis' Maesteg Merthyr
> Dos veces cribado   9/6
> Una vez   9/-
> Menudo   5/-
> Coke para herrerías (Davis Patent Coke) 15/-

Part of a price list for coal from Oakwood Colliery, June 1888; Fry, Holman & Fry were the colliery's Cardiff sales agents. The list was prepared for a Spanish customer and states that Davis's double-screened steam coal was available at 9s 6d. per ton, small coal at 5s per ton.

> **Elders' Navigation Collieries**
> LIMITED,
> AGENCIES:—
> LIVERPOOL — ELDERS' NAVIGATION COLLIERIES, Ltd., COLONIAL HOUSE, WATER STREET.
> SOUTHAMPTON — NISBET & CO.
> HAVRE — CUNARD STEAMSHIP CO.
> PARIS & NANTES — S. LOIRET & Ch. HAENTJENS.
> HAMBURG & ANTWERP — ELDER, DEMPSTER & CO.
> ROTTERDAM — P. A. Van ES & CO.

During the years 1900 to 1915, Elder's Navigation sold steam coal from Oakwood and Garth through their agencies in the major European ports.

> SOLE AGENTS:
> **LYSBERG LIMITED,**
> Cambrian Buildings,
> Cardiff.
>
> Tel. Address — "LYSBERG, CARDIFF."
> Tel. No. — 3280, Private Branch Exchange.
>
> **CELTIC COLLIERIES Ltd.**
> REGISTERED OFFICE:
> 21, MERCHANTS EXCHANGE, BUTE DOCKS, CARDIFF.

From 1916 until the decline of the export trade, both colliery companies in the Llynfi Valley sold their coal through Messrs Lysberg of Cardiff.

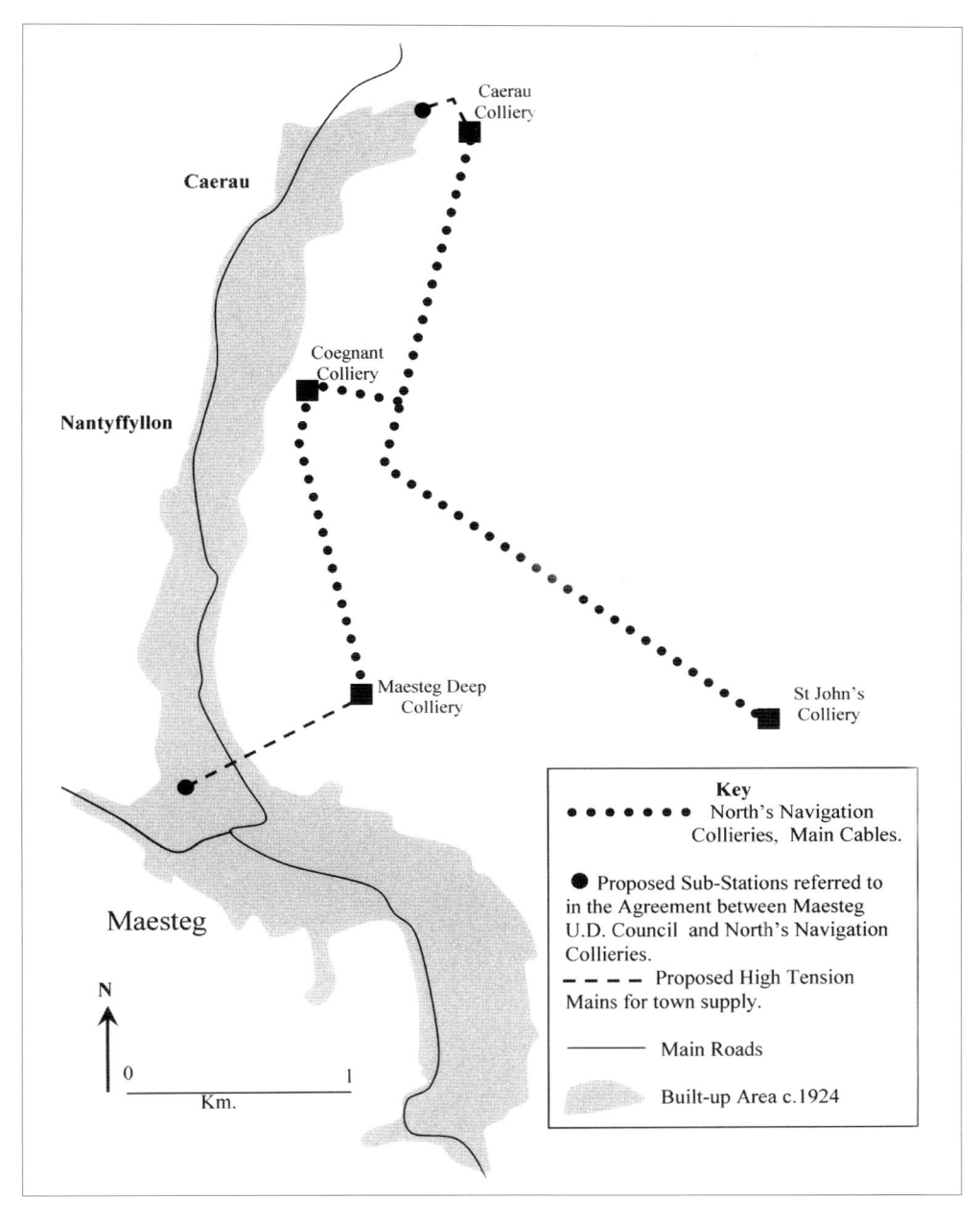

North's Navigation Collieries Ltd: Electrical supply, from aound 1924. By 1920 North's mines were supplied with electricity from power stations at Caerau and Coegnant collieries. The power station at Caerau Colliery, for example, produced 1.5MW from two turbo alternators. There was the 'nucleus' of a third power station at St John's and electricity was also produced at Maesteg Deep. The company's four mines were connected by a transmission line carried on wooden poles. By 1924 the local council had made an arrangment with North's to supply electricity for public use. From the proposals shown on the map, one spur connected the colliery 'grid' to a sub-station near the present-day sports centre, and a shorter spur carried power from Caerau Colliery to a sub-station on Caerau Road. Source: *Map referred to in the First Schedule of the* Maesteg Electricity: Special Order, *1924*

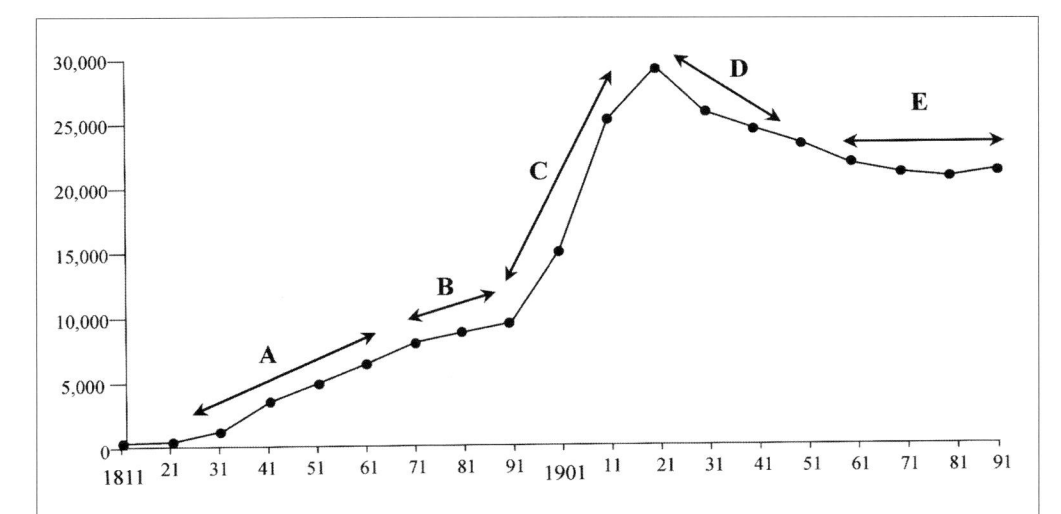

Population Trends 1811–1991 *Source: census.*

Code: A: Steady growth as the iron industry develops.
B: Growth checked as iron and tin trades decline, some migration to USA.
C: Spectacular growth as large mines are opened, especially in the upper valley.
D: Large-scale out-migration as older pits close permanently and other mines are affected by foreign competition and the world-wide trade depression. After the Second World War there was less demand for Llynfi Valley coal, and fewer workers were needed due to mechanisation.
E: With the decline of employment in local mining, new light industries grow up in the area and a residential function develops as people travel daily to new jobs created in the Bridgend and Port Talbot journey to work areas. Population varies little in forty years.

Some Significant Dates

1828: Opening of Dyffryn Llynvi & Porthcawl Railway, Maesteg Ironworks.
1839: Opening of Cambrian (later Llynfi) Ironworks.
1861: Opening of steam-hauled Llynvi Valley Railway.
1885: End of ironmaking.
1889: Formation of North's Navigation Collieries Ltd.
1890: Sinking of Caerau Colliery commences.
1900: Development of Garth Colliery by Elder's Navigation Collieries Ltd.
1904: Development of Coegnant Colliery.
1908: Sinking of St John's Colliery commences.
1924: Local miners' leader Vernon Hartshorn becomes a Cabinet Minister.
1930: Closure of Garth Colliery and Maesteg Deep.
1931: 2,500 local job losses during the year.
1947: Nationalisation of the coal industry.
1985: The closure of St John's Colliery marks the end of coal mining locally.

Industrial Prosperity and Civic Pride. The enlarged town hall with its clock, and the distinctive council offices on the right both date from 1914 and reflect the growing prosperity of the town in the years before the First World War.

With the further development of local collieries and the consequent growth of population, Maesteg became a major shopping centre by 1914. In this view of Commercial Street in about 1920, the junction with Talbot Street in the distance is dominated by the Co-operative building of 1910, which was one of the first reinforced concrete structures in Wales. At the right of the photograph is part of Laviers' department store.

Present-Day Buildings Associated With North's Navigation Collieries

Above left: The former colliery offices of North's Navigation, erected 1908, at the corner of Talbot Street and Castle Street. *Inset:* detail of the company initials above the main entrance.
Above right: View of the Colonel North Memorial Hall, around 1905. Designed as a miners' welfare hall and library, it was opened in March 1899, three years after the sudden death, aged fifty-four, of the founder of the colliery company.

Miners' Institutes and Libraries. Five large miners' institutes were built in the Llynfi Valley. Caerau, Nantyffyllon (Coegnant), Cwmdu (St John's), and Garth were linked to their respective collieries, North's Hall was centrally placed near the town hall. They were referred to locally as 'libraries' and each consisted of a hall with recreation areas, a library and a reading room. Three of the five buildings remain: Cwmdu (above left), which opened in 1924, and now houses a light engineering unit; Nantyffyllon (above right), which opened in 1926, has been refurbished to provide a range of facilities for the local community and part of North's Hall is used as an amusement centre.

The Remarkable Colonel North

The rapid growth of the Llynfi Valley during the years 1895–1915 was largely due to the investments made by Colonel North and the colliery company he formed in 1889. From fairly humble beginnings, John Thomas North accumulated a large fortune during the 1880s through a combination of good luck and astute dealings in the South American nitrate trade.

Unlike other coal-owners in South Wales in the late 1880s, North was a global operator and his colliery company in the Llynfi Valley was a major component in an early example of a multinational organisation with interests in South America, Australia, and Belgium.

Some years later, by coincidence, the mineral wealth of the valley attracted another global operator to the district: Sir Alfred Jones of the Elder Dempster Shipping Co., whose collieries at Garth and Oakwood formed part of a major enterprise with links to the Canary Islands, the West Indies and West Africa.

Right: Vernon Hartshorn and Political Change in the Llynfi Valley. Mid-Glamorgan Constituency.

General Election 1910	By-Election 1910
Sir S.T. Evans QC (Liberal): 13,175	F.W. Gibbins (Liberal): 8,920
G.H. Williams (Unionist/Cons.): 3,382	V. Hartshorn (Labour): 6,210
Liberal Majority: 9,793	Liberal Majority: 2,710

Vernon Hartshorn's by-election result in 1910 marked the emergence of the Labour Party in the Llynfi Valley and the end of Liberal domination in the district. Some years later, in 1918, Hartshorn entered Parliament, unopposed, for the new Ogmore Constituency.

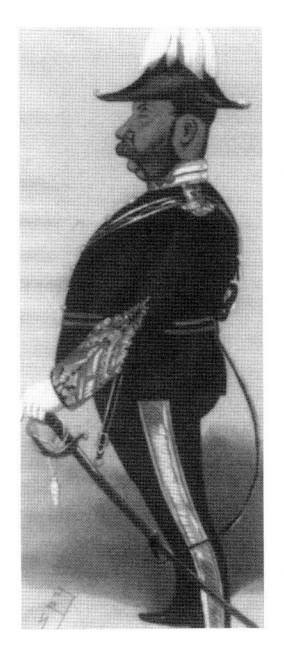

Far left: Colonel John T. North, 'The Nitrate King', larger-than-life speculator, sportsman and socialite. *From* Vanity Fair *caricature, Nov. 1889*

Left: John Thomas North, founder of North's Navigation Collieries, self-made industrialist, financier and philanthropist. *At Avery Hill, Eltham, Kent, 1890*

SOME PROMINENT FIGURES IN THE LLYNFI VALLEY COAL INDUSTRY.

Above left: Vernon Hartshorn (1872–1931), former miner and check-weigher, Miners' Agent for the Maesteg district, chairman of Maesteg UDC, Member of Parliament, Cabinet Minister.

Above right: Sir David Llewellyn (1879–1940), chairman of North's Navigation Collieries (1889) Ltd, 1924–40.

Below left: H. Seymour Berry, (Lord Buckland) 1877–1928, chairman of North's Navigation Collieries (1889) Ltd, 1918–24, chairman of Celtic Collieries Ltd, 1916–24.

Below right: Sir Alfred Lewis Jones 1845–1909, founder of the Liverpool School of Tropical Medicine, principal partner Elder Dempster Shipping Co., founder of Elder's Navigation Collieries Ltd.

THE LLYNFI VALLEY COAL INDUSTRY – SOURCES OF INFORMATION

PUBLISHED TEXTS AND ARTICLES

R. Page Arnot (1975) *South Wales Miners* Cardiff
A.P. Barnett & D. Willson-Lloyd (1920) *The South Wales Coalfield* Cardiff
James Barrow (1872–3) 'The Llynfi Valley Mineral District' *Transactions of the South Wales Institute of Engineers, 8*
Harold Blakemore (1974) *British Nitrates and Chilean Politics 1886–1896* London
Harold Blakemore (1962) 'John Thomas North, the Nitrate King', *History Today 12*
David Burrell (1995) *The Nitrate Boats* Kendal
Colin Chapman (1998) *The Vale of Glamorgan Railway* Usk
David Davies (1961) *Ty'r Llwyni* Port Talbot
Ll. Davies & O. Davies (1924) *South Wales Coals* Cardiff
P.N. Davies (1978) *Sir Alfred Jones, Shipping Entrepreneur Par Excellence* London
P.N. Davies (1973) *The Trade Makers, Elder Dempster in West Africa 1852–1972*, London
Elder Dempster & Co. (1901) *Ocean Highways* Liverpool
H. Francis & D. Smith (1980) *TheFed*. London
A.G. Hopkins (1973) The *Economic History of West Africa* London
G. Howells & C. Rees (1999) 'Pneumoconiosis: A Study of its Effect on Miners' Health in South Wales, 1900–1980', *Nursing Standard, Vol.13, No.26*
Graham Humphrys (1972) *Industrial Britain: South Wales* Newton Abbot
D.R.L. Jones & J. Lyons (1997) *The Garth Colliery Disaster of 1897* Maesteg
Philip N. Jones (1969) *Colliery Settlement in the South Wales Coalfield 1850–1926* Hull
Samuel Lewis (1842) *A Topographical Dictionary of Wales* London
Sir Digby Mackworth (1843) *A Report for the Proprietors of the DLPR* Bristol
Kenneth O. Morgan (1981) *Rebirth of a Nation: Wales 1880–1980* Oxford
Dafydd Morganwg (1874) *Hanes Morganwg* Aberdare
National Union of Mineworkers (1985) *St John's Colliery, Maesteg: The Alternative to Closure* Maesteg
William Phillips (1924) *The South Wales Coal Buyers' Handbook* Cardiff
Gwilym J. Rees (1997) *Tondu House* Sully
Brinley Richards (1982) *History of the Llynfi Valley* Cowbridge
Clive Smith (1985) *Railways of the Llynfi Valley* Port Talbot
Peter Stead (1969) 'Vernon Hartshorn: Miners' Agent and Cabinet Minister' Glamorgan Historian, Vol. 6 Barry
William Williams (1895) *A Sanitary Survey of Glamorganshire* Cardiff
J.T. Woodhouse & S. Dobson (1860) *Maesteg Iron Works* London
The South Wales Coal Annual, 1905-17 Cardiff

Government/Local Government Publications

Glamorgan County Council (1951) *Development Plan Area No.1, Report of Survey* Cardiff
Local Act of Parliament   3 Edw.7. Ch.xi *North's Navigation Collieries (1889) Limited Act 1903*
Reports of HM Inspectors of Mines, Cardiff & Swansea Districts, 1888, 1902–09.
Report of the Royal Commission (1926) *TheCoal Industry (1925), Volume I* HMSO
Report of the Royal Commission *TheEmployment of Children and Young Persons in Mines and Manufactories 1842*
Mines Dept, *List of Mines* 1891–1950 HMSO
A. Woodland & W. Evans (1964) The *Geology of The South Wales Coalfield, Part IV* HMSO

Contemporary Newspapers and Journals

The Bridgend Chronicle (Bridgend Reference and Information Centre)
The Cambrian (Swansea Central Library)
The Cardiff Shipping and Mercantile Gazette (Cardiff Central Library)
The Central Glamorgan Gazette (Bridgend Reference and Information Centre)
The Glamorgan Advertiser (Bridgend Reference and Information Centre)
The Glamorgan Gazette (Bridgend Reference and Information Centre)
The Mining Journal (National Library of Wales, British Newspaper Library, Colindale)
The Syren and Shipping Illustrated (British Newspaper Library, Colindale)
The Times Digital Archive (National Library of Wales)

Contemporary Documents

The Cambrian Iron & Spelter Co.: a Memorial, 8 June 1843, PRO (C54/12916)
Coegnant Lodge Disputes Books, South Wales Coalfield Collection, University College, Swansea (MNA/MUM/L/23/127-8)
Files of Dissolved Companies, Celtic Collieries Ltd, PRO (BT31/3181/65244)
Files of Dissolved Companies, Maesteg Merthyr Colliery Company Ltd, PRO (BT31/1904/7721)
Letters of James Bicheno to the Marquess of Bute regarding Chartism in Maesteg, 1840, NLW (Bute Estate 2, L83/411, L83/471)
Letter from Morgan Davies, Llangynwyd, to the Marquess of Bute regarding the miners' strike at Coed-y-Garth Colliery, Maesteg, September 1845, NLW (Bute 2 L90/178)
Llynvi Tondu & Ogmore Coal & Iron Company, Correspondence, WGRO (D/D Gn/I/16-29)
North's Navigation Collieries, Colliery Report, March 1890, GRO (D/D X 209/2)
North's Navigation Collieries, Estates' Book, NLW (Brinli 33/10)
North's Navigation Collieries, Ledger, GRO (D/D PD 45)
North's Navigation Collieries, Short Working Book, GRO (D/D PD 46)
North's Navigation Collieries, Stock Book, GRO (D/D PD 44)
North's Navigation Collieries, Notice to Shareholders, April 1914, UoN (P1 F10/5/4/12)
North's Navigation Collieries, Notice to Shareholders, November 1916, UoN (P1 F10/5/4/42)
North's Navigation Collieries Ltd., PRO (COAL 34/600)
North's Navigation Collieries Ltd., PRO (COAL 38/553)
Poster advertising the Mineral Lease of Mynydd Caerau, c1857, WGRO (NAS Gn/E 13/3)
Report of the Directors of the Cambrian Iron and Spelter Company, 1840, NLW (LL/MISC/226)
Report of the Mineral Resources of Troedyrhiw Farm, Cwmfelin, November 1844, GRO (DXiu 1)

Report on Maesteg, Margam and Other Works Belonging to Robert Smith and Company, May 1840, Mushet Correspondence, Gloucestershire Record Office (D2646/151)
South Wales Coal Owners' Association, Caerau Dispute 1894-6, NLW (CC22)

ABBREVIATIONS

NLW – National Library of Wales, Aberystwyth
GRO – Glamorgan Record Office, Cardiff
PRO – Public Record Office, The National Archives, Kew
UoN – University of Nottingham, Dept of Manuscripts
WGRO – West Glamorgan Record Office, Swansea

INDEX

Abraham, William (Mabon), 67
Admiralty List, 78, 79, 93, 134
Allen, James Hodgkins, 17, 20
Amalgamated Association of Miners, 66, 67
Anticline, Maesteg, 13, 119, 141
Avery Hill Eltham Kent, 39, 153

Barrow, James, 18, 26, 27, 29, 36, 48, 56, 106, 115
Baths Pit-head, 89, 96, 99, 100
Batters, George, 25
Bedford, John, 16
Berry, H. Seymour (Lord Buckland), 47, 53, 154
Beynon, David, 68
Bicheno, James, 34, 64
Board of Guardians, Bridgend, 85, 86
Bowring, John, 11, 31, 74
Boyd-Harvey, John, 41, 44, 45, 68
Brogden & Sons, 23, 26, 36, 106, 135, 136
Brogden, Alexander, 23, 26, 66
Brogden, John, 23
Buckland, William Henry, 34, 35
Bute, Marquess of, 34, 64, 65
by-election 1910, 153

Caerau Building Society Ltd, 43
Caerau, growth of, 43-45
Cambrian Combine, 47, 53, 106, 115
Cambrian Iron & Spelter Co., 11, 19-21, 31
Cambrian Miners' Association, 67, 68
Canary Islands, 49, 50, 153
Celtic (Admiralty Coal), 53, 79
Celtic Collieries Ltd, 53, 79, 83, 106, 115, 131, 135, 154
Certificates of Earnings, 33
chartism, 64
coal ranks, 78, 143
coal seams, 14, 15, 141, 142, 144, 145
coke production, 50, 79, 106, 107, 109, 110, 112
collieries

Blaenllynfi, 20, 24
Bryn Rhyg, 132
Caedefaid (No.9 Level), 24, 25, 44, 57, 92, 135, 146
Caerau, 15, 42, 43, 45, 60, 67, 68, 84, 93-97, 135, 138, 146, 149
Caerau No.3 Pit, 43, 93, 94, 146
Coed y Garth, 21, 64
Coegnant, 17, 43, 67, 68, 70, 76, 98-105, 135, 138, 146
Crown Pit, 18
Cwmdu (see St John's)
Davis's Pit (see Oakwood)
Dyffryn Madoc, 20, 28, 127, 136
Garnwen (No.12 Level), 29, 130, 136
Garth (see Garth Merthyr)
Garth Merthyr, 23, 28, 29, 48, 50, 57, 58, 69, 80, 83, 84, 106-109, 135, 136, 146
Gin Pit, 20, 28, 54, 55, 127, 136
Maesteg Deep, 41, 59, 60, 83, 110-114, 135, 136, 146
Maesteg Merthyr (see Oakwood)
Nant y Crynwydd, 20
No.1 Pit, 18
Oakwood, 24-26, 29, 48, 55, 56, 59, 69, 83, 115-118, 135, 146
Office Level, 20
Quarry Level, 132
Tygwynbach (No.11 Level), 128, 136
Tywith (Tychwith), 21, 23, 26, 128, 136
St John's (Cwmdu), 44, 84, 89, 119-126, 135, 138, 146
Scwd Level, 23
Sheppard's Pit, 18, 19
colliery accidents:
  Gin Pit 1863, 54, 55
  Oakwood Colliery 1872, 55, 56
  Garth Colliery 1897, 57, 58
  Maesteg Deep Colliery 1904, 59, 60
colliery advertisements, 80, 147
colliery employment totals, 135, 138

Colquhoun, James, 33
company shop (see Truck System)
Corr, Superintendent, 65
Cory Brothers, 83, 106
Cox Idris, 86
creeper mechanism, 102
Cripps, Sir Stafford, 87
Cwmdu Board of Health, 35, 36
Cwrt-y-Mwnws Farm, 23, 111

David, Llewellyn, 16
Davies, Morgan, 65
Davis, William, 24
Davis's Merthyr Colliery Co., 25
Defence of the Realm Act, 72
Deutches Kohlen Depot, 46
Dobson, Samuel, 18
Dyffryn Llynvi & Porthcawl Railway (DLPR), 17, 22

Elder's Collieries Ltd, 52, 135
Elder Dempster Shipping Co., 49
Elder's Navigation Collieries Ltd, 48-53, 135
electricity supply, 149
evictions, 86
explosions (see colliery accidents)

Foster-Brown, T., 27
French Navy, 46
furnace ventilation, 116
Furness, Withy & Co., 48

Galloway, Prof. William, 50
Garth Merthyr Steam Navigation Collieries, 29
Grand Canary Coaling Co., 50

Hampton, Charles, 21
Halliday, Thomas, 66
Hartshorn, Vernon, 70-74, 153
Harvey, Sir Robert, 39, 45
Hospital, Maesteg General, 75
house coal, 80, 112
Hubbuck, George Parker, 32
Humby, James, 29
Hunger March, 86

Imperial Navigation (Admiralty coal), 78, 79, 134
industrial disputes (local)
    Maesteg Ironworks 1835, 63
    Coed y Garth Colliery 1845, 64, 65
    Llynfi Ironworks 1853, 66
    Caerau Colliery 1894–6, 67, 68
    Non-Unionism 1927, 73
    Boys' Strike 1942, 75
industrial disputes (national/regional)
    1898, 69
    1912, 72
    1921, 72
    1926, 72, 73
    1972 1974, 76
    1984-5, 76
Iquique, Chile, 139, 140
Ironworks
    Cwmdu, 18
    Garth, 21
    Llynfi (New Works), 19, 20
    Maesteg (Old Works), 18
    Tondu, 20, 128
Italian State Railways, 46

Jones, Sir Alfred Lewis, 48, 49, 52, 154
Jubilee Slide, 142

Knight, Revd Robert, 65
Kylsant, Lord (Sir Owen Philipps), 52, 53

Lemon, R.P. & Co., 18, 136
Lewis, Dr James, 35
Liverpool Nitrate Co., 39
Llewellyn, Revd Pendrill, 34, 35
Llewellyn, Sir D.R., 47, 154
Llwyni Farm, 16
Llynvi Coal & Iron Co. Ltd, 24, 26, 33, 136
Llynvi Iron Co., 20
Llynvi & Tondu Co. Ltd, 29, 36, 40, 136
Llynvi Tondu & Ogmore Coal & Iron Co. Ltd, 26-28, 136
Llynvi Vale Iron Co., 20, 24, 136
Llynvi Valley Railway (LVR), 22, 23
Lockett, G.H., 45
London 'coal ring', 42

Mabon's Day, 67, 69
Macgregor, Alexander, 32
Maesteg Distress Relief Committee 1878, 28, 29
Maesteg District Distress Fund 1926, 72, 73
Maesteg Merthyr Colliery Co., 25
Malins & Rawlinson, 64
Metcalfe, Stephen Wright, 55
Metcalfe Street, 128
Mining Areas Relief Fund, 85
Moelgilau fault, 13, 141, 142
Moffatt, George, 24, 28, 78

National Unemployed Workers' Movement (NUWM), 85, 86

National Union of Mineworkers (NUM), 75
Nitrate King (see North, John Thomas)
North, John Thomas, 37-42, 152, 153
North's Memorial Hall, 42, 152
North's Navigation Collieries (1889) Ltd, 37-47, 81, 135
North's Navigation Internal Railway, 113, 121
North's Navigation Smokeless (steam coal), 79
Nystagmus, 61, 62

Park Coal Co. Cardiff, 112
Parry, Inspector, 86
Patch, No.3, 18
Patent Galvanized Iron Co., 21
Pen-y-Castell Fault, 19, 98, 132
Pillar, Thomas, 32
pit-ponies, 124
pneumoconiosis, 61, 62
population trends 1811–1991, 150
Port Talbot Docks, 42, 46, 50, 137, 139, 140
Port Talbot Railway, 42, 140

Ranger, William, 35
Roe, John Phanuel, 36, 55
Royal Mail Group, 107
Russian Navy, 46, 134

Saklatvala, Sapurji, 74
Sheppard, Charles, 18, 19, 26
Sierra Leone Coaling Co., 107

silicosis, 61
sliding scale agreement, 67
Smith, John Joseph, 29, 33, 36, 37, 40, 41, 44, 45, 47
Smith, J. Wentworth, 47
Smith, Robert, 64
South Wales Miners' Federation (SWMF), 69, 71, 73, 75
Spelter Works, 17, 105
strikes and lock-outs (see industrial disputes)

Tenerife Coaling Co., 107
Tondu House, 41
Toncwd Row, 17
tram circuit, 102
truck system, 30-33

unemployment rate, 84
Union Castle Shipping Line, 46, 134

Vale of Glamorgan Railway, 42
Victoria Investment Corporation, 48, 135

Waddle Fan, 24, 50, 107, 115, 116
Washery, Maesteg, 113, 114
War of the Pacific, 38
Western Navigation Collieries Syndicate, 40
Woodhouse, John, 18, 23
Workmens Compensation Acts, 61

If you are interested in purchasing other books published by Tempus,
or in case you have difficulty finding any Tempus books in your local bookshop,
you can also place orders directly through our website

www.tempus-publishing.com